PHIL TAYLOR-GUCK

ALTERNATIVE INVESTMENTS

HOW TO SAFELY DIVERSIFY IN TIMES OF UNCERTAINTY

Re^think

First published in Great Britain in 2023
by Rethink Press (www.rethinkpress.com)

Contents

Introduction

My interest in alternative investments was sparked by an encounter while on holiday with my family in Dubai. I got talking to another businessperson at our hotel and discovered that he was involved in a deal to buy a private plane. He was bringing together several high-net-worth individuals who would each chip in a proportion of the sale price and then receive income from renting it out to other high-net-worth individuals. As an entrepreneur with an interest in a large number of businesses, I was intrigued. How would the consortium work, I wanted to know? How was the money protected? What would happen if one of the investors wanted to sell? The man eloquently answered all my questions, but I couldn't help noticing that, in the main, he seemed to be doing his best to put me off the idea. I asked him why. 'Alternative investments aren't for everyone,' he replied with a shrug. 'Besides, meeting another person in a bar while on holiday and being offered an unbelievable investment opportunity should always be a red flag.'

We both laughed at this and he was, of course, right. Alternative investments are, without a doubt, firmly at the riskier end of the market for a range of reasons. For a start, the regulations around them are much less strict than they are in traditional markets and with some asset classes there is nothing to protect the investor at all. This, in turn, leads to one of the most pressing problems. These investments attract a disproportionate number of fraudsters and chancers – the type of people who really would sidle up to others at a bar and offer them the opportunity of a lifetime.

Despite all of this, I was intrigued. One of the most enjoyable parts of my job is putting deals together and working with other entrepreneurs

to help them reach their goals. Was there something here for me, I wondered? Certainly, the
timing seemed right. One of the other aspects
of alternative investments is that, although they
present a greater risk, there is also the chance
of greater returns. As any investor will attest,
the opportunity to grow, or even just maintain,
wealth in the current environment is dismal.
Indeed, if you were to describe the economic
recovery post-Covid-19, the word you'd most
likely use is 'painful'. In 2022, UK inflation
hit a forty-one-year high of 11%, far exceed-
ing even the gloomiest expectations.[1] Prices
followed a steady trajectory upwards in food,
transport and energy, squeezing households
and businesses. In September of the same year,
the pound hit an all-time low against the dollar following the disastrous mini-budget that
marked the brief tenure of chancellor Kwasi
Kwarteng. It plunged almost 5% to $1.0327,
the lowest since the UK went decimal in 1971.[2]
In the months that followed, there was little
comfort to be gained from the International
Monetary Fund, which forecast that Britain will
be the only major industrialised country to see
its economy shrink in 2023.[3]

The year 2022 has been dubbed 'one of the worst years ever' for markets, and not just in the UK.[4] The US stock market experienced an 18% loss, which ranks as the seventh worst since the 1920s, behind the Great Depression of 1931 and the Global Financial Crisis of 2008. Similarly, the US Bloomberg Aggregate Bond Market Index had its worst year in its forty-year history, showing a total return of −13% in 2022, while the benchmark US government bond was down 15%. In the UK, the situation has been just as bleak. UK investors have helped beat another record with the rate they are ditching UK stock funds. Almost £8.4 billion flowed out of UK-focused equity funds, the worst in eight years, over fears that the economic downturn in the UK would last longer than elsewhere thanks to a tight labour market, low business investment and weak exports.[5] For comparison, there were also £2.65 billion in outflows from other European stock funds, £1.17 billion from North American funds and a similar amount from Asia Pacific funds.[6]

It has also been a bad time for fixed-income investments. Global bonds were down by −17%

and global bonds linked to an index slumped by −22%. UK index-linked bonds suffered at a greater rate, down by −21% and −31% respectively.[7] Even gold, long seen as a reliable hedge against inflation, was down −3% in US dollar terms.

Faced with a trading environment like this, it more than makes sense to cast around for a better way to make our money work and protect our wealth. What better way then, than to take a leaf out of the book of the super-rich and emulate some of their investment practices? *They* don't seem to be unduly impacted by the downturn. A big part of this is because they don't follow the same investment strategies as the rest of us. They've worked out where the best places are to put their cash to yield the highest return to support their millionaire lifestyles. In short, they have access to alternative investments. These investments frequently offer significantly higher returns than the traditional markets and 81% of wealthy investors include them in their portfolios.[8] They are not just dabbling, either. The portfolios of high-net-worth investors (a category for those with a fortune of $30 million or more) are made up of 50% of alternative assets. It's a similar story, although to a lesser extent, with millionaire and multi-millionaire investors who allocate 26% of their investments to this asset class.

Alternative assets have yet to make significant inroads into the portfolios of those with lower disposable incomes. These assets make up just 5% of an average retail investor's portfolio. Most people who are used to investing in stocks and shares are, quite rightly, cautious about this less familiar option. But this is not a niche market. The total alternative investments under management (AUM) are estimated to hit $17.2 trillion in 2025.[9]

Interest in alternative assets is not a new phenomenon, either. Their potential first began to be explored as far back as the Fifties, in line with the growing interest in the diversification of investment portfolios after economist and Nobel laureate, Harry Markowitz, developed the Modern Portfolio Theory (MPT).[10] The push towards diversification was largely in response to the roller coaster ride of the markets over the

previous half-century and the series of spectacular falls, not least the 1929 Wall Street Crash.
Markowitz advocated building a portfolio that
maximised the level of returns while quantify-
ing the level of portfolio risk. Diversification
seemed the most sensible option to spread
investments across different asset classes – the
perceived wisdom being that such a portfolio
will experience fewer losses than a portfolio
based on a single asset. When an investor has
several kinds of assets, they are less vulnerable
to shifts in the market. Where the bottom falls
out of the market for one asset, the rest of the
portfolio will support it.

While MPT has since come under criticism for
its reliance on a standardised set of assumptions about market behaviour that doesn't sit
easily in a constantly changing financial climate,
the idea of diversification has caught on. Indeed,
since the Fifties, interest in diversification has
grown, as have the opportunities in new asset
classes. Another market crash, this time in 1973,
opened the way for pension funds to invest in
a broader range of assets, thanks in great part
to the US government's Employee Retirement

Income Security Act which allowed this move. In the same year, the British Rail Pension Fund began investing in artwork to diversify its interests, eventually putting £40 million (or 3%) of its holding into art holdings.[11] Since this time, there has been increased interest in investing in real estate, via a range of mechanisms. We have real estate investment trusts (REIT), real estate mutual funds, buy-to-let, and opportunities to invest via crowdfunding. Hedge funds have become popular among high-net-worth investors who use them as a means of diversifying risks and sharing costs. Meanwhile, there has been a huge growth in investment in luxury assets such as whisky and wine.

In recent times, technology has also played a role in bringing alternative investments to a broader range of people to form a vital part of their diversified portfolio. Almost anyone can open an account with an online broker or investment app, and many of these trade alternative investments as well as traditional securities. Developments in fractional investing (or tokenisation) split large assets up into smaller pieces, so it is now possible to buy a stake in everything from an office complex to a supercar. This growth in digital trading has inevitably attracted a new generation of investors: individuals who have grown up with a smartphone in their hands and who are comfortable buying and selling investments online. Today, 80% of young investors are actively looking at alternatives in the hope of realising above-average returns and are allocating three times more of their investment portfolio to alternatives than older investors.[12]

There is – often justifiably – a lot of negative information about alternative investments. Yet, while there are risks and a fair few sharks out there, I don't believe investors should completely steer clear. Educating yourself is key. There are opportunities, but to take advantage of them, you will need an understanding of the economic drivers and what to look out for and what to avoid.

Since my chance meeting in Dubai, I have put together a team of experts in alternative investments and have been working on some intriguing opportunities. As with all my new business ventures, I have learned a lot along the way. I have written this book to share the information I have gained. It is the book I wish I'd had when I started. If you are new to alternatives and looking to diversify your portfolio, it will help you understand the risks involved in the various options and how to mitigate them. Since thorough due diligence is essential for every investment, I will share the questions you should be asking about opportunities and where to go to find the information you need. Likewise, I will show how crucial it is to assess the credibility of the team behind the deals on offer. While I will mention several specific investments here, from artwork to collectables to shipping containers, my goal is not to recommend one over the other. Far from it. I simply want to make people aware of the pros and cons of each one in terms of value creation versus risk. It is up to individual investors to evaluate what is best for them and their own needs.

Above all, I aim to take some of the mystery out of this asset class so it can be considered on its merits and take its place alongside more mainstream investments. As with any investment, it is up to an individual to decide upon their appetite for risk and how many alternatives they'd like in their portfolio.

ONE

What Is An Alternative Investment?

For any investor to succeed, they need a firm grasp of the financials to navigate a path going forwards and, as far as possible, some certainty that their money is safe and in the right place. Individuals are often suspicious of alternative investing because few understand what is included in the asset class or, indeed, what constitutes an alternative investment. A broad definition would be an investment that doesn't fit into the conventional mould, such as stocks, bonds or cash investments, and cannot be easily converted into cash. However, there is a lot more to alternatives than that. This is one of the largest and most dynamic asset classes. Initially, the alternative umbrella included private equity and debt, commodities such as gold, as well as real estate, infrastructure and hedge funds. Over time, these early types of alternatives have become more mainstream and a new group of investment opportunities has emerged to join them. This new group includes everything from art to collectables, life settlements and litigation finance, and has earned the collective moniker of 'exotic' since these items are relatively less common. This means that alternatives are now a very broad asset class indeed.

Since the goal of any shrewd investor is to build resilience into a diversified portfolio to protect capital for the long term, I'll begin by exploring all of the assets that meet the 'alternative' criteria, from mainstream investments to exotics.

Mainstream alternative assets

You may already be familiar with many in this category. This is a group of investments which includes private equity, private debt, hedge funds, real estate, infrastructure and commodities.

Private equity

Private equity funds are said to offer one of the most significant opportunities for retail investors who are new to the alternative investment market, not least because historical returns show that this asset class is generally resilient to market cycles (certainly more so than many public market indices). According to data provider Preqin, around half the investments in alternatives, $6.9 trillion, are in private equity funds.[13]

This is in itself a broad category, referring to any capital investment made into private companies or those not listed on a public exchange such as the London Stock Exchange. The category can be further subdivided into subsets, including:

- Venture capital, focusing on business startups and early-stage ventures

- Growth capital, where investment is used to help more mature companies expand or restructure

- Buyouts, where one company or one of its subsidiaries is bought outright

The success of investment into private equity will very much depend upon the principals in the firm managing the investment. Traditionally, private equity involves more than a simple funding deal, where one party invests in another with the expectation that the business receiving the capital will make the best use of it. This is a partnership-style arrangement. Private equity firms provide additional intellectual capital benefits such as the mentoring of founders in the investments being backed, helping them source new talent and advising on growth strategies, all of which are aimed at accelerating growth. Funds turn a profit when the private equity firm liquidates its stake, either by taking the portfolio company public via an initial public offering (IPO) or by selling it to another company.

Private debt

Investments that are not financed by banks (eg, with a bank loan) or traded on an open market are known as private debt. The 'private' part of the title is, however, a little misleading. Rather than referring to the borrower of the debt, it describes the investment instrument itself. Private debt is used by companies needing additional capital to expand and the companies that issue such capital are known as private debt funds. They make their money through interest payments and the repayment of the original loan.

Hedge funds

Participation in these pooled investment funds remains largely only available to high-net-worth individuals and institutional investors via endowments, pension funds and mutual funds, all of whom have to pass strict investment criteria. The returns can be high, but frequently dependent on sometimes risky investing strategies. These strategies include leverage, which is borrowing to invest, and short-selling, where fund managers look to profit from falling share prices. There's also market neutral, where a fund seeks to earn above-average returns regardless of the prevailing market conditions, and volatility arbitrage, a statistical strategy that attempts to profit from the difference between the forecasted future price volatility of an asset and the implied volatility of options based on that asset.

Real estate

Real estate is well known as the world's biggest asset class and putting money into bricks and mortar is still seen as one of the most *accessible* forms of alternative investing. Many experienced investors are drawn to real estate because it has characteristics that are similar to bonds and equity investments. When individuals invest in buying property, the resulting cash flow from tenants paying rent resembles the benefits from bonds. There is also an expectation of capital appreciation, where the long-term value of the asset will rise, just as happens with equity.

One of the most significant challenges of real estate investing is valuation. There are various methods, including capitalisation, discounted cash flow and sales comparable, which all have their pros and cons. To be successful in this category of investment, it is crucial to understand each option and to know in which circumstances they are best deployed.

Infrastructure

Infrastructure describes physical assets that underpin an economy such as roads, hospitals and schools, as well as electricity transmission, water supplies and the physical equipment that enables the internet to function. Until recently, most infrastructure investments were made by the government. This has now evolved into combined public-private partnerships where investment firms and major institutions such as pension funds play a role in large developments. One area that is currently getting particular attention is any investment in infrastructure which will help the transition to net zero. Investments into the renewable energy infrastructure offer investors exposure to the physical assets that generate renewable energy or help electricity grids balance the intermittent output of resources that capture the energy of the sun, wind or hydro.

Many countries around the world have adopted energy policies and laws that encourage investment in renewable energy. Within each market, there are various subsidy regimes which offer different risks and rewards. Investments in renewables still come at a higher risk than government bonds, but the returns can also be higher. This is a growth area in the alternatives market, with firms looking at new sources of financing such as public-private partnerships that leverage private capital to support their goals.

Commodities

Although technically another 'real' asset, commodities are an asset class of their own. We are talking here of mostly resources, materials or substances that occur naturally on Earth such as agricultural products, oil, natural gas and precious and industrial metals. All of these commodities have been traded for thousands of years and the raw materials are often engineered, processed or refined into more complex materials to realise their economic value, which can rise and fall according to supply and demand. The higher the demand for a particular commodity, the higher the price and the greater the investor profit. Commodities such as gold are considered to be a hedge against inflation because they are not sensitive to the shifts of the private equity markets and generally outperform other asset classes.

So far, so familiar. What, then, is included in the newer alternatives class, the so-called 'exotics' I mentioned earlier?

Exotic alternative assets

Investments in this category cover a wide spectrum. To give you a sense of their scope, I've selected eight different options.

Aircraft leases

This is the asset class that first got me interested in alternatives and it is easy to see why there is a growing interest in aircraft leasing. Sales of private jets are at their highest point since records began, with 1,399 deals closed in 2022, up 2% from the previous year.[14] These planes are getting plenty of air time, too, with private plane use also soaring to the highest level on record, with 3.3 million take-offs in a year, which is 7% more than the previous high, recorded before the pandemic.[15] It's not just corporates and a select group of the super-rich who are using private jets, either. A number of charter companies are popping up that allow 'ordinary' people to book seats on an empty leg or a repositioning flight where a plane is returning to base after a one-way flight. It's not as expensive as you might think, either. To charter a plane from the UK to the South of France will cost around £13,000[16] which, while still a lot of money, is pushing the asset class into the realms of being more accessible. The increasing normalisation of luxury travel is seen to be behind much of the demand.

The opportunity for alternative investors lies in the huge capital outlay for an aircraft. Any aeroplane, private or otherwise, is extremely expensive to buy. Planes are either bought directly from manufacturers such as Airbus or Boeing, or via sale-leaseback agreements with major airlines on existing fleets. The global aircraft leasing market was valued at $167.8 billion in 2021 and is forecast to grow at a rate of just under 8% until 2029.[17]

The market for aircraft leases was perceived to be quite complex, but in line with the growth of the sector, the growing need for capital investment is attracting a new breed of investors, including private equity funds and alternative investment managers. The process is also becoming correspondingly easier to manage.

Art and art finance

The year 2022 was a record-breaking year for art sales, despite the slump in the general financial markets. Andy Warhol's silkscreen series *Shot Sage Blue Marilyn* sold for an eye-watering $195 million, Paul Cezanne's *La Montagne*

Sainte-Victoire went for $137.8 million, and even the tenth-best seller, René Magritte's *L'Empire des Lumières* made a spicy $79.8 million. As an asset class, contemporary art continues to outperform the S&P 500, as it has done so every year for twenty-five years. Between 1995 and 2020, the S&P 500 returned an average of 9.9% a year, while contemporary art achieved 14.3%.[18]

Million-dollar price tags for major artworks inevitably create a lot of interest, although, for any would-be investor looking to snap up an entire piece, it's not an option for the faint of heart or, indeed, the light of pocket looking at the prices above. The good news is that there are several alternative options at far more palatable prices, thanks to art funds, art-lending services, and funding or insurance products related to fine art. Most recently, art has become an even more attractive investment opportunity, thanks to the growth in interest in tokenisation, which is the process of taking the cost of a big-ticket item and breaking it down into smaller pieces. When investors buy a proportional stake in a piece of artwork, their ownership of it is then officially recorded on the blockchain. New

York-based company Masterworks has been at the forefront of this trend, buying up highly sought-after works of art and securitising them. Investors can now buy a fractional investment in paintings by famous artists like Pablo Picasso, Claude Monet or Banksy. There is no need to stump up $195 million to own an Andy Warhol anymore. Masterworks sold 99,825 shares in one of the artist's paintings of Marilyn Monroe for just $20 each. Investors make their money when the investment is sold. The returns can be substantial, with some tokenised works of art achieving returns of 30% or more.

Collectables

By definition, a collectable is any object regarded as being of value or interest to a collector, but assets in this category also act as a store of value when stock markets are volatile, bond markets are subject to inflation and fiat currencies depreciate.

For clarity, the goal of investing in collectables is, or should be, viewed purely from a financial perspective and have nothing whatsoever to do with whether or not individual investors have an interest in, or affinity to, the intrinsic value of an investment. Many investors may already own, or have inherited, collectables such as art, stamps or coins. To this end, they may have very strong views about the art, stamp or coin market and derive much pleasure from their collection. Collections like these are classed as 'passion collections', where profit is a secondary consideration – if it is considered at all. The focus in the context of the alternatives is on investing in collections that will become a functioning part of an investment portfolio. Those who invest in collectables purchase and maintain physical items in the hope that the piece in question will become worth more than the sum originally paid for it because of its rarity and/ or popularity. Categories of collectables include:

- Baseball cards
- Coins
- Fine art
- Stamps
- Rare wines
- Toys

- Vintage cars
- Whisky

According to Knight Frank's Luxury Investment Index,[19] fine wine and watches are at the front line of alternative investments in collectables when it comes to the size of return, with each producing a return of 16%. Other high performers include art (+13%), rare whisky and coins (both +9%). Coloured gemstones, one of the world's oldest forms of investment assets, have seen some of the biggest price jumps in their 5,000-year history over the past few decades. Popular stones such as rubies, sapphires and emeralds have increased between 5% and 8% year-on-year since 1995.[20] Lesser-known gemstones such as tourmaline, aquamarine and alexandrite have seen consistent and stable price jumps over this period, too.

Cryptocurrency

Almost everyone will be familiar with the term cryptocurrency, particularly the most well-known one: Bitcoin. There are currently thousands of listed coins and tokens. The Financial Action Task Force defines these digital (or virtual) currencies as, 'a digital representation of value that can be digitally traded and functions as (1) a medium of exchange; and/or (2) a unit of account; and/or (3) a store of value, but does not have legal tender status.'[21] These currencies are not issued or guaranteed by any government or central bank and can only be accepted as payment for goods through the mutual agreement between the vendor and customer.

If you are familiar with crypto, you are most likely so for all the wrong reasons. Many of these 6,000 cryptos have generated headlines because of the spectacular rises and falls in their value. Suffice it to say, if you wish to base your alternative investment strategy around buying and selling these assets, the best advice is to be prepared for a few shocks. The reason for including crypto here is not to recommend speculating with Bitcoin. No, where the future of crypto lies (and the opportunity as an alternative investment) is in the technology that is *behind* their currencies: blockchain. A blockchain is an electronic database that consists of a collection of data packets, or 'blocks'. When a block is filled, it is connected to the next block, hence the term blockchain. Unlike traditional databases, this data chain is entirely decentralised, making it a highly safe way to securely transmit and store information. No single person or organisation has control or ownership over the information that is recorded on the blockchain. As well as substantially reducing the possibility of fraud, the technological breakthrough is more efficient and less costly to operate. As already outlined, blockchain is key to making the art market more accessible, since it allows large assets to be tokenised and safely offered to a large group of investors. It is early days, but blockchain holds the key to fractionalising a large number of asset classes from real estate to supercars, as investors safely and securely buy a portion of big-ticket investments. Market projections predict that by 2027, up to 10% of global GDP could be stored on blockchain,[22] expanding into a $16 trillion business opportunity. The trade in securities and 'real' assets will be central to this growth.

Intellectual property

Although an intangible asset, intellectual property can be owned, traded, leased and rented in a similar way to physical property. In this case, the asset is a patent, copyright or licence around a unique idea or a resource upon which a licence has been created. Investors can, of course, buy shares in companies that own certain intellectual property (IP), but the alternative investment opportunity is where investors buy shares that have been created in the IP itself. In a similar process to the fractionalised opportunities already mentioned, investors can buy a piece of a patent and potentially receive a share in the resulting dividends, royalty or lease income.

A range of industries rely on IP, including mining, music, technology, entertainment, healthcare and pharmaceuticals. Thus, for example, investors could make returns out of licensing land rights to those who wish to develop a site or to benefit from the by-products that are farmed or mined on it, such as timber or coal. Those who invest in the IP of the output of musicians can collect fees every time a track is performed or used in a movie or game. There is currently a total of about $3.2 billion invested in music royalty funds.[23] Someone who invests in a patent based on development in technology will benefit when it is licensed to manufacturers and developers who want to make use of the advance in their products.

Rates and fees in this asset class vary considerably. They are based on several variables, many of which are to do with the usual business advantages and disadvantages such as supply and demand, exclusivity and geography. Recorded royalties and dividend rates can be as low as 1% and as high as 50%. For context, a benchmark from one marketplace found that music royalties delivered a 12% yield.[24] There is also a range of investment options to choose from: IP rights can be leased for an annual fee, sold for a lump sum or exchanged for equity in a business venture.

Life settlements

Death, like taxes, is one of life's most certain events. The UK's life insurance market is well established and of a significant size. It was valued at $178.71 billion in 2021. It is forecast to grow by more than 7% in the period between 2020 and 2025[25] as many individuals recognise that life insurance policies are an important way to protect family interests when the inevitable happens. What is perhaps less well known is that there is a secondary market for life insurance policies known as 'life settlements'. Here, life insurance policies are purchased by a third party at a discount to face value, without any changes to the insured, for an amount that exceeds the cash surrender value of the policy, but which is lower than the death benefit. The policyholder receives an immediate cash payment, while the investor continues to pay the premiums and will receive the death benefit upon the death of the insured.

Why you may ask, would individuals seek to sell their premiums ahead of when they are needed? After all, they began paying into their life insurance policy with the intention it would cushion the blow for their families upon their death. The truth is, many people have no choice but to either let their policies lapse or to sell them back to insurance companies when finances become unexpectedly tight. This is a particular problem during a depressed economic cycle. During 2022, more than a third of the over-fifty-fives (39%) said their outgoings exceeded their income every month.[26] Cashing in a life insurance policy via life settlement is often their best option. This is particularly pertinent to retirees, who have limited options to increase income or raise cash. Life settlements allow them to make a decent level of return on their initial investment and are certainly a more attractive option than selling their home or agreeing to an equity release scheme. There is the option of surrendering the life insurance to the company that provided the policy, but this is not the most efficient way to make money. Individuals who agree to life settlement rather than surrendering a policy for its cash value receive roughly four times as much as the cash surrender value. It's an attractive asset for investors, too, because they can get a decent rate of return, usually in the double digits, with no loss of principal. Once again, this is another investment opportunity which benefits from fractionalisation, with larger policies being split up into smaller investment policies.

Litigation finance

Everyone knows that when lawyers get involved, things get expensive. What is not as widely known is that ordinary investors can benefit from these big bills, thanks to litigation finance. This arrangement makes a great deal of sense, too. When complex cases cost upwards of £50,000 and can drag on for months, or even years, there are few people with pockets deep enough to pursue them. Many litigants will need to seek out alternative sources of funding.

Litigation finance can be used for a range of different cases, including raising funding for legal action related to consumer or commercial disputes, as well as intellectual property and patent disputes, malpractice, accident, contracts, class action and negligence. It is even used for divorce cases. One of the UK's most expensive and high-profile divorces was funded with litigation finance.[27] Litigation finance company Burford Capital became involved in the $480 million, high-drama battle between Russian oligarch Farkhad Akhmedov and Tatiana Akhmedova after Akhmedov lost against his ex-wife in their original court case in 2016. The flames of the lengthy dispute were further fanned when he hid over $100 million of assets to avoid paying the large settlement, sparking an expensive five-year legal battle that largely centred around a super-yacht which changed custody several times during this period. It's been said that there are no winners in divorce cases, but Burford did quite nicely out of it. They profited by more than $70 million from its litigation finance investment.

It should be said that most legal cases funded by litigation funding are nowhere near as fascinating as this divorce. Indeed, many are pretty boring. That said, the litigation finance market has been forecast to grow by nearly 7% between 2020 and 2026, to eventually turn over $60 billion per annum. While these investments were previously the preserve of hedge fund managers and high-capital businesses, fractionalisation is more common today and individual investors can invest directly via certain platforms.

Shipping containers

We all have something in common. It doesn't matter if you relax by scrolling through the news on a touch screen, by sipping your favourite dark Columbian roast coffee, by taking time out on your comfortable Italian leather sofa, or any combination of these scenarios, the chances are high that a large number of the objects you surround yourself with have travelled many miles to be part of your daily routine. An estimated 90% of the world's goods travel the oceans to get to us.[28] That includes foodstuff, household goods, technology and clothes. An estimated 60% of items on that list get placed in giant steel containers to be shipped. The rest, mainly commodities like oil or grain, are transported after being poured directly into the hull of ships.

Shipping containers are another alternative investment asset that can be owned, rented or leased to companies shipping goods. Outside funds are sought because the shipping companies that transport hundreds of containers at a time tend to put their resources into buying the vessels rather than the containers themselves, so they often lease shipping containers rather than buy them outright. This presents investors with an opportunity to invest in shipping containers and reap a return of more than 12% a year.[29]

* * *

As this chapter shows, there are multiple alternative assets available. There are also many ways to gain exposure to alternative investments. At the simplest level, if you have the means, it is possible to directly buy an asset at full price. We've also seen how many alternative assets are now available through a process of tokenisation, which is something that is expected to become more widely available in the years to come.

TWO

The Pros And Cons For Individual Investors

The alternative asset market is a fraction of the size of the mainstream markets, yet it is gathering momentum. According to the Securities Industry and Financial Markets Association (SIFMA), the global equity market capitalisation was $124.4 trillion in 2021, while the outstanding value of the global bond market is $119 trillion.[30] During the same period, the alternative investment market reached $13.32 trillion. What is most remarkable is that it has almost doubled since the 2015 level of $7 trillion,[31] having grown at the rate of *seven times* that of traditional asset classes. And it is still growing. By 2026, it is forecast to grow to $23.21 trillion.[32]

Given the lacklustre state of the post-pandemic markets and the potentially outsized returns offered by some alternative investments, it would be an easy leap in logic to imagine that the growth curve in this asset class may even exceed expectations. The fact that it has not done so (and is not expected to, either) is a testimony to the caution of investors – and rightly so. Alternative investments are not for everyone. While there is, indeed, a broad spectrum of opportunities on offer and a potentially decent level of return, the adage still stands: the higher the return promised, the higher the risk. The extremely optimistic outlook for the alternatives market indicated by the figures above doesn't tell the full story or properly describe the roller coaster ride of alternative investments in the past decade or so. Alternative assets are vulnerable to big shocks. In the two years before the 2008 financial crisis, global alternative assets under management (AUM) nearly doubled, from $2.9 trillion to $5.7 trillion.[33] However, in the aftermath of the credit crunch, the market slumped alarmingly.

Often, an alternative asset will seem to be enjoying tremendous growth and then, almost overnight, its fortunes will change entirely, frequently leaving investors with a large holding they are unable to sell or monetise in any way. Take shipping containers as a prime example. Traditionally, these hard assets have not fluctuated in value in the same way as other financial assets and have looked like a steady bet. An increase in global trade has caused demand to rise steadily since 2010 as, like so many other alternatives, this asset class has consistently grown at a faster rate than GDP. For a while, in the wake of the pandemic, shipping containers were seen as an exceptionally good opportunity when there was a shortage of containers, with many trapped in the wrong ports after the trade was abruptly halted during successive lockdowns. With the supply chain in crisis and people wanting goods, the market looked very promising indeed. Fast forward to mid-2022 and entirely the opposite was true. The global economy was facing the opposite problem: *too many* shipping containers. A downward shift in consumption appetites, perhaps fuelled by fears of an impending economic downturn, meant many container ports were full. In November 2022, the Drewry composite World Container Index, an important benchmark for container prices, fell to $2,773 per 40-foot container, 73% lower than the peak in September of the previous year.[34] Anyone with a large portfolio of shipping container leases would have been in a very perilous position.

The clear message is this: any individual seeking to diversify into alternatives needs to go into this with both eyes open and take the time to understand all the complexities around what they are buying. In this chapter, I have listed the advantages and disadvantages of investing in alternatives. As you will see, the number of advantages is strikingly small compared to the number of disadvantages. And, this is before you get to the increased potential for fraud and mis-selling, a subject to which I have devoted an entire chapter.

Advantages

Potential for outsized returns

Let's be entirely honest; we are attracted to alternatives because of the potential for incredible returns. As we saw from the brief run-through of some of the opportunities on offer in the previous chapter, while some alternatives achieve returns broadly in line with the FTSE 100 average return of 7.8%[35] or the S&P 500 average of 10%,[36] many can achieve double that, or sometimes even more. That's impressive by any measure, and particularly so at a time when the main markets are not performing well.

Like any investment, alternatives derive a great part of their value through the simple laws of supply and demand. Investors will look to profit from buying into an asset such as art or wine when demand for the asset is increasing and while the supply remains fixed, or they'll jump in when the supply of the asset is growing more slowly than demand and, all being well, will do so for a period well into the future. If demand goes up faster than supply, then the price will rise. The opposite is, of course, also true. If demand collapses, then the price will fall precipitously. The point is that there is a potential for significant double-digit gains, which is far more than what is currently available in the traditional markets.

The value in alternatives can also be derived from the right to future income streams, cash flows or rents. Think here of investments that might offer decent revenues in the months and years to come, such as intellectual property rights, life insurance and litigation settlements. Often, the extent of the future cash flows is not fully known when the investment is sold or may be uncertain. There is even a chance it might not happen at all. As a result, access to such investments is often at a significant discount. When the barrier to entry is low, anyone who is well informed about their potential can profit handsomely.

Another potentially outsized return can be had from spotting products, services or businesses that are about to disrupt a market. It can be a risk to get in on the action before anyone knows which way things will go, but the returns can be extraordinary. Think of some of the best-known disruptors such as Amazon, Airbnb, Uber and Starling Bank. Each one has played a role in displacing the traditional players and transforming the way things have been done in their respective sectors. Imagine what returns you could have had if you had been able to put money in during an early venture capital (VC) round.

The holy grail for all investors in alternatives is to spot, and then take full advantage of, a lucrative market opportunity well ahead of everyone else. When we can use our special skills, knowledge or expertise to single out a particular asset class that offers financial gains far over those to be had from the more mainstream markets and we get that call right, it can feel pretty good. The returns can be exceptional, too.

New investment opportunity

Until recently, private investors were almost entirely blocked from most alternative investments. This could either be because of a high barrier to entry because few ordinary individuals could afford tens of thousands of pounds to invest in big-ticket investments, or because funds offering certain investments had strict entry criteria only permitting the super-rich to take part. The favoured few were a small category extending to high-net-worth individuals or private family offices. To enjoy the status of being a high-net-worth investor in the UK, an individual would need to earn at least £100,000 per annum or hold $250,000 in assets, excluding their primary residence, insurance or pension policies. In the US, to achieve a similar distinction, investors would need to have a net worth of $1 million or more, more than $200,000 in net income (or $300,000 together with their spouse) or hold a financial industry licence. Rules in the EU have been equally strict and the bloc also requires that a person (or entity) has a deep insight into the market and experience dealing with securities before gaining access to many alternative investments. Their professional and educational background may also be considered to evaluate their eligibility.[37]

Most people cannot hope to meet such exacting criteria, so what has been behind the recent explosive growth in the alternatives market? The number of high-net-worth individuals has not doubled in less than a decade, nor have we seen a rapid uptick in the number of financial licensees. The opening up of the markets to a broader group of investors has, in great part, been driven by opportunity and need. The poor performance of the markets, coupled with higher inflation and an ageing demographic, is forcing many (particularly those close to retirement) to reassess their investment strategy and seek out wider options. This clear demand from investors for better and more reliable returns has not gone unnoticed by established investment groups, from JP Morgan and BlackRock to HSBC. These firms now run huge teams offering alternative investment solutions and strategies to help investors to diversify portfolios with a mix of private equity, infrastructure and real estate in a development dubbed 'the democratisation' of investment. Alternative investments which would previously have only been available to the super-rich are being packaged into regulated mutual funds and sold through traditional channels which do not demand such strict entry criteria. As a result, alternatives are infinitely more accessible to a much wider group of investors.

The more widespread take-up of alternatives has also, in great part, been facilitated by technology.[38] As already noted, several platforms have tokenised opportunities where investors can access alternatives with smaller sums of money. The internet has become an invaluable tool for those without professional knowledge because it helps to educate them about *all* the available investment options. A plethora of new technology platforms has also opened the way for private investors to seek out new ways to increase their returns by allocating funds to private equity investments. Digital wallets have opened access to entirely new asset classes such as cryptocurrency, while mobile trading platforms offer real-time insights into investments.

Reading this, you may have concerns that such growth will inevitably turn out badly for some less experienced investors and you'd be right.

We will talk more about how to avoid getting caught out later in this book. For now, I will note that the democratisation of alternatives has not gone unnoticed by the authorities, who do not want a new 'Wild West-style' frontier opening in the carefully regulated financial world. Governments around the world are looking at ways to *safely* broaden investment opportunities for retail investors. There is also an understanding that support will be needed for less experienced investors, who are often less knowledgeable and less able to tolerate losses than the professional investors or wealthy individuals who have historically dominated this market.

Individual governments are acutely aware that they can't allow things to move too quickly when it comes to opening this market, but it's a balancing act, because they also need to stay ahead of where the market wants to go. We are currently in a 'consulting stage', which indicates that some movement will be forthcoming. In early 2022, for example, the Financial Conduct Authority (FCA) launched a consultation to see whether it was prudent to market long-term asset funds (LTAF) to a wider group of retail investors in the future. The review was in response to complaints from some quarters that the 'consumer journey' towards high-risk investments was too smooth and there was too much misleading promotional material which encouraged the unwary to pile into dangerous investments. The UK financial regulator's response has been tough, but fair. It has announced plans to crack down on misleading adverts that promote investing in high-risk products. However, it has been proposed that LTAFs are made available to more investors, albeit with restrictions. Restricted investors will need to sign a statement agreeing not to invest more than 10% of their assets into illiquid assets or non-readily realisable securities. There are also recommendations around longer redemption periods, higher levels of disclosure and stronger governance features.

The relaxing of some of the rules echoes moves by the European Union to change the European long-term investment fund (ELTIF) framework to broaden investment opportunities for retail investors. In the US, the Asset Management

Advisory Committee (AMAC) successfully lobbied the Securities and Exchange Commission (SEC) to open access to private equity, private debt and private real estate investments for retail investors. Changes to the US pension scheme already mean employees can include private equity investments within their retirement savings.

The message here is that the market is changing and being made available to a broader group of investors. However, it is early days, and while private investors should benefit from more impressive returns with alternatives, they still do not receive anything near the same protections as when they invest in the traditional markets.

Fun

The final big tick in the 'advantages' box is fun – a word that is seldom used in conjunction with investing. I strongly believe that fun should at least get a mention as a factor in alternatives. Investing in something outside of the normal asset classes gives investors a chance to put their money into something that reflects their interests. If you are already a collector then you will recognise the thrill of the hunt of searching out, and then securing, a rare item. It can be almost as satisfying as owning it. There is, of course, an obvious caveat here. Being interested in an asset is not the same as knowing all the potential pitfalls as an investor or an invitation to ignore the advice of experts or the underlying financials.

Disadvantages

Illiquid

Stocks and shares are liquid investments that can be rapidly bought and sold on the open market with relative ease. In comparison, assets in the alternative investment market have always been subject to longer lead times. Indeed, one of the biggest criticisms of alternatives is that they are illiquid and can tie up an investor's money for substantial periods. The investment cycle for some funds is as short as one year, but others require money to be committed for extended periods of up to five, or even ten, years. In private equity, for example, the idea is to buy into a company to support its improvement over the subsequent five to seven years (sometimes even longer). This long-term outlook is fine for institutional investors who may have several private equity investments all at different stages in the life cycle. However, this long-term structure can present challenges to the individual investor with a more limited portfolio, particularly if, for example, such an investor is a retiree who might prefer ready access to their funds. Investors need to understand that not only are alternatives inherently riskier, but they also won't have access to their money for some time.

Many alternatives come with limitations on withdrawals by imposing 'lockup' periods, during which time the invested capital cannot be liquidated. These lockups further split into two categories: hard and soft lockups. In a hard lockup, investors cannot withdraw capital at any time within a specified period. The soft lockup option allows for the withdrawal of capital, but these withdrawals are subject to a penalty fee.

On the plus side, liquidity is becoming less of an issue. The trend towards tokenisation makes it easier to trade assets with other collectors. As it stands, these alternatives are currently still far less tradable than publicly tradable assets, but expect to see huge strides to address this with a new generation of secondary trading markets for tokenised assets.

High fees, investment thresholds and tax

The minimum investment threshold is generally higher with alternative assets than with traditional stocks and shares. Not only that, but these alternatives also tend to have a higher cost associated with them. The fee structure of hedge funds, for example, is frequently '2 and 20'. Here, the investor pays 2% per annum, and 20% of the profit above a previously agreed benchmark goes to the fund manager.

Then there is the question of tax. The amount of tax to be paid will depend on the type of asset involved, how long it is held and the level of the investor's income. Some alternatives might be subject to favourable tax treatments to encourage investment, but many are not. The tax status of this type of investment can be complicated and it is important to get advice from a professional to make sure you are assessing your investment liabilities correctly.

Insurance can be another major hidden cost component in certain alternative classes such as art or collectables, not least because there is considerable risk involved when it comes to damage or ageing of the objects in question. If physical assets have been acquired and are kept in the home or business premises of the investor, it might be assumed that they will fall under an existing coverage. This is, however, not always the case – particularly with extremely valuable items. If they do fall under existing coverage, it is more than likely any policy will vastly undervalue the asset and would not be sufficient to fund a replacement should it be needed. In cases like this, insurance needs to cover a variety of scenarios, according to the item/s in question, including fire and water damage, earthquakes or theft. Policyholders may incur additional expenses to comply with insurance pre-conditions to protect items, such as fees to install specific security systems or fire protection. There could also be clauses restricting how an asset is displayed to protect it from theft, as well as precautions to prevent any deterioration in quality. Finally, there may even be title insurance to make sure the items in question are free from claims from previous owners or collectors.

Lack of performance data

The less mainstream an alternative investment, the generally less understood they are and this can mean investors are exposed to often complex risks. As we've seen, alternative investments represent a broad category and are all so different. Real estate is nothing like art. Art is nothing like life settlements.

Verifiable data is an essential tool for investors when mapping out their portfolios. Take the market for collectables as a case in point. While the market might sound like fun, particularly for those with an interest in specific collectables, it can present a real investment challenge, too. Investors need a high degree of expertise in the collectable to spot rising markets and some collectable markets in particular are quite niche, so there will be a lack of reliable performance data. At times, the rise in the value of some alternative collectables won't seem to make sense at all. Collectables have no intrinsic value, so they are subject to the tastes, moods and perceptions of buyers and sellers, which are notoriously fickle and can diminish overnight. In 2021, Pokémon cards soared in popularity, partly due to the pandemic lockdowns which fuelled a sense of nostalgia for carefree childhoods from days gone past. The Pokémon Company had to print nine billion cards to keep up with demand and maintain the supply. Investors snapped up unopened packs in the hope of finding a rare shiny Pokémon card to flip for a decent profit. At the height of the Pokémon-mania, actor and professional wrestler Logan Paul spent over $5 million on a PSA Grade 10 Pikachu Illustrator card, which he wore around his neck on his WWE wrestling debut at WrestleMania in Arlington, Texas. He repeated the stunt with a Charizard card, which he proudly displayed at his boxing bout with

Floyd Mayweather. Not surprisingly, following such a peak of excitement in 2020 and 2021, the price of the cards has begun to decline.

Some alternative assets have unique risk factors. In aircraft leasing, for example, it is challenging to correctly estimate the residual value of any aircraft. The rate of depreciation will also have an impact, since the collateral itself supports the loan or lease. If the value of the aeroplane declines more quickly than the value of the lease, it can expose the investor to additional credit risk.

Investors need to do their fair share of home-work to understand the sources of risk which can come from understanding a true valuation. They also need to be sure of the liquidity of the investment and the amount of time their cash will be tied up and be prepared for difficulty in accurately forecasting supply and demand or cash flow. It can, for example, be complex to assess risk levels on pooled structures (or commingled funds) because there simply isn't enough information. This can leave investors vulnerable. As we learned from the financial crisis of 2008, it is not unheard of for unscrupulous financial managers to actively use window dressing to disguise risky assets to make them look a lot more lucrative than they are.

Lack of regulatory protection

Many alternative investments are not regulated, and when this is the case, there are fewer protections for investors. They will not, for example, be covered under the Financial Services Compensation Scheme (FSCS), which would pay compensation in the event of a default by a management company. However, if a provider advises on a regulated investment such as an equity fund and the firm fails, investors may be eligible for compensation via the FSCS. Ditto, if there has been misconduct or evidence of mis-selling or fraud from the authorised arranger of the fund. Very often though, if investors do find their stake being wiped out and the investment was unregulated, there is little that can be done.

Don't forget, a large part of the reason why there is so little information available about alternative investments is that companies offering these opportunities don't have to provide the same level of information as their mainstream counterparts. That the regulatory environment is nowhere near as intensive should raise alarm bells, but that's not to say it won't be in the future. As detailed earlier, this sector is under scrutiny from the authorities to weed out bad actors. In August 2022, the FCA sent out a 'Dear CEO' letter, warning industry players that it is scrutinising whether products are being offered to the right clients.[39] Firms that could not show they were taking 'reasonable steps' to ensure clients were taking appropriate risks would receive further attention.

For now, the accepted advice remains: if an investment is unregulated, only consider investing as much as you can afford to lose entirely.

Previous good performance is not a guarantee of excellent future returns

The fact that returns are not guaranteed is a truism of any investment and this includes alternatives. Even investments that appear to shine, showing many years of outsized growth, can experience a spectacular fall from grace.

In the introduction to this chapter, I mentioned the roller coaster ride of certain alternatives since the financial crisis. This is particularly the case with some of the more well-known asset classes in this category, which have not delivered what was hoped. A prime example is hedge funds. In the period between 1997 and 2007, an equally weighted hedge fund index achieved a cumulative return of 225%, comfortably beating an equally weighted stock and bond portfolio, which delivered 125%. Following the financial crisis, the trend for hedge funds to generate substantially larger returns than portfolios of stocks and bonds flipped. Between 2008 and 2016, hedge fund indexes fell short, returning

25% versus a 70% return from a stock and bond portfolio.[40] Things have not improved since then. Hedge funds continued to trail the market in the subsequent period of 2017 to 2020.[41] The under-performance has been blamed on heightened regulatory oversight and central bank interven-tion. This may have impacted the type of trading that hedge fund managers can do, potentially limiting their performance. In addition, inves-tors have demanded lower fees, which has put pressure on many hedge fund firms.

Private equity has had a similarly rocky time in recent years. While investors continue to pour money into global private equity buyout funds (more than $1 trillion since 2017), lured by the oft-repeated promise that these funds produce the best returns and far outperform the stock market, the reality warrants closer inspection. An analysis by the lobby group, American Investment Council, found that in the ten years until September 2020, private equity funds produced a 14.2% median annualised return, net of fees, compared with 13.7% for the S&P 500. Public pension funds invested in private equity achieved worse returns than the S&P, at 12.8% net of fees.[42] Yes, private equity is still (mostly) outperforming the stock market, but not by much. Again, the shift in gear has been blamed on moves by the authorities to force more transparency in the market. Another factor is issues with IPOs, with many extremely disappointing private-equity-backed exits. The IPOs of Deliveroo, Uber and Lyft are just a few of the much-hyped exits that have not lived up to expectations by failing to reach target prices.

The real estate, or buy-to-let, market has also seen a marked downturn in returns, even though property values have largely continued to rise following the financial crisis. This is, in great part, because this particular asset class has found itself firmly in the sights of politicians who have imposed a succession of punitive tax changes – not just upon the income derived by landlords, but also on the gains of any who decide to sell up and abandon the market altogether. In the UK, landlords are no longer able to claim tax relief on mortgage interest which, for many, means their rental income no longer covers the cost of the property and brings their yields to below zero.

All of the above brings us to the obvious question: if the returns of these alternatives are largely in line with stocks and bonds, yet also carry more risk and lower liquidity, where is the real advantage? Investors may get lucky with the alternative assets they include in their portfolio and receive exceptional returns, but equally, they may not. As with all investments, there are no guarantees that alternative assets will perform well. They may not move with the market and when the rest of the market is trending upwards, they can sometimes head in the opposite direction.

Questions over the legal and ethical status

There are occasionally concerns over the legality of certain alternative investments. One of the investment classes I didn't cover in the previous chapter was medical cannabis. In recent years, the legal cannabis industry has become big business around the world and has fallen under the gaze of many investors in alternatives. Both recreational and medicinal cannabis has been legalised in Canada since October 2018, translating into a market worth more than $4 billion in sales annually. In the US, various states have taken the same path and legalised both recreational and medicinal use of the drug. The US cannabis industry was worth $10.8 billion in 2021 and is expected to show an annual growth rate of nearly 15% over the next decade.[43] The UK's regulatory stance towards cannabis is more complex and, at the time of writing, occasionally contradictory. Medicinal cannabis was legalised in November 2018, partly in response to several high-profile cases recounting huge breakthroughs in the treatment of children suffering from severe forms of epilepsy. Since then, several 'cannabis companies' have been listed on the London Stock Exchange and Alternative Investment Market, although none are 'pure plays', meaning they also have interests outside of marijuana. Many more companies are building a reputation in legal medicinal cannabis, making the UK one of the largest producers in the world. However, while it might appear that the UK's stance is softening, access to legal medicinal marijuana is limited. Most GPs are not allowed to prescribe it unless they are listed on the General Medical Council's Specialist Register. Meanwhile, the drug is still illegal for recreational use and the current Home Secretary has indicated that she is receptive to reclassifying it as a Class A drug.[44]

Another consideration for some investors is the ethics behind the assets they fund. In mainstream investing, many fund managers rule out being involved in tobacco, weapons or gambling. Any investor who takes more control over their portfolio by allocating more money to alternative investments might like to weigh up the ethics behind their investment choices. An individual who feels passionately about, say, green issues, may not wish to invest in airline leases, since private planes have been cited as one of the world's worst polluters.

*   *   *

There is no doubt that alternative investments reward smart, knowledgeable investors with outsized returns. But, as these pros and cons show, there is a reason why, until now, alternative investments have mainly been the preserve of experienced investors and the super-rich; the former group can thoroughly investigate the pitfalls and the latter group can afford to lose their stake. It's not simply a case of the so-called 'elites' keeping the best opportunities for themselves.

Alternatives present a more complex trading environment when compared with mainstream investments and expose investors to a higher level of risk. The onus is on investors to do their analysis to understand possible returns in a market where it is very difficult, or even impossible, to judge which alternative investment is going to perform well under the prevailing market conditions. This level of opacity can be a fairly daunting prospect for anyone who is new to the market or who has previously relied on financial advisors to do the due diligence.

As we will see in the next chapter, there is one more, significant reason why investors may shy away from alternative investments: a heightened potential for fraud.

THREE

Buyers Beware: How To Spot Scams

I nvestment scams. The people who get duped into them are just naïve, right? With a bit of financial savvy, it's pretty easy not to get caught out. Or so the thinking goes. Except, this isn't true. Consider the most famous investment scandal in recent memory, the Ponzi scheme masterminded by Bernie Madoff, which took the dubious accolade of being the *largest ever* Ponzi scheme when it was revealed in December 2008. By that time, Madoff had taken $65 billion in investments. The money was not stolen from naïve investors with no idea of what they were doing. The roll call of people that lost money to Madoff included many top Wall Street financiers and sophisticated investors, as well as celebrities such as Kevin Bacon, Steven Spielberg and basketball legend Sandy Koufax, all of whom could no doubt afford savvy advisors. Everyone missed the scam – even the regulators. Somehow, the SEC failed to spot that Madoff was secretly using cash from new investors to pay handsome returns to old ones, even though, in some cases, these returns were by far a long way in advance of anything available elsewhere. Blue chip bank, JP Morgan, ran Madoff's account with millions upon millions of dollars passing through it and there were no suspicious activity reports. In the end, it was the financial crisis of 2008/9 that brought it all to a head. As the markets crashed, spooked investors rushed to make withdrawals from Madoff's funds and the scheme quickly ran out of money to give them. Madoff revealed the extent of the fraud when he called a meeting with his sons and admitted that it had all been a lie. The family lawyer then contacted regulators and they alerted federal prosecutors and the FBI.

The reason for highlighting the Madoff case is to show that, while alternative investments are often highlighted as susceptible to fraud, it is not always immediately obvious what the scam artists are up to. The onus is very much on individual investors to have their wits about them and to *always* ask questions. Bernie Madoff was a skilled fraudster who used his charisma and credibility to convince early investors. As the scale of the returns became known, more investors jumped aboard the gravy train, no doubt becoming less cautious the more they heard about how well others had done. Sadly, this is not an isolated story. There is a huge range of ways that the unscrupulous try to defraud investors, with some being more easily detected than others. Among the firms that trumpet unbelievable returns which then turn out to be fraudulent, there are examples of:

- A complete failure to properly assess the suitability of investments for both retail and professional clients.

- Clear conflicts of interest, especially where dominant shareholders have made material decisions in disregard of governance processes or the impact on investors with smaller stakes.

- No adequate systems to manage funds operating with high leverage, which therefore exposes investors to higher risk.

- No systems and controls are being implemented to mitigate the risks of market abuse.

- Nothing being done to prevent inappropriate remuneration policies for fund principals that are detrimental to the interests of investors.

The rest of the chapter will cover details of just some of the scams that have been uncovered over the past few years, with a few thoughts on what might have been done differently, and whether there was any chance that investors could have spotted the criminal intent before they parted with their cash. It is by no means an exhaustive list of what might happen, but it should give you an idea of the lengths to which fraudsters will go to help investors part with their cash.

Style over substance never pays[45]

It is often believed that if an opportunity has the endorsement of celebrities, then it has to be legit. The truth is, this is not always the case, as many alternative investors have found to their cost. Indeed, the crossover of alternative investments with so-called 'pop culture' is occasionally a real issue, particularly in the digital world. The explosive growth in crypto and non-fungible tokens (NFT) has, in part, been fuelled by the endorsement of celebrities, athletes, politicians and influencers, only for some assets to burn out because they have not made the potential risks clear. Fortunately, there has been a clampdown on misleading schemes. Kim Kardashian was fined $1.26 million by the SEC for promoting cryptocurrencies without disclosing that she'd been paid to do so,[46] while Elon Musk has been widely criticised for using memes and Twitter to pump bitcoins like Dogecoin and Shiba Inu.

This phenomenon is not just reserved for the virtual world. It's been used in more down-to-earth investments, too. Take the story of the huge number of people who were tempted to invest in holiday cabanas and apartments across the Caribbean and Brazil on the back of celebrity endorsements combined with slick events and glossy brochures. The development was the brainchild of Essex businessman, David Ames, who was behind the Harlequin group, an international network of resort development companies. Investors who attended the presentations by the charismatic Ames, held at golf clubs, conferences and exhibition centres across the UK, had no idea that he was a two-time bankrupt following failed ventures selling garden furniture and windows. His enticing message was further bolstered by his promises of celebrity associations with the lavish holiday schemes which were to be built across seven resorts. Wimbledon champion Pat Cash was signed on to endorse tennis academies at the resorts, while golfer Gary Player was in charge of designing a course and, according to Harlequin's promotional YouTube video, none other than Liverpool FC was to be associated with football training at the resorts. Senior Caribbean politicians also lent their weight to the scheme.

More than 8,000 investors paid a £1,000 reservation fee and a 30% deposit, half of which went towards Harlequin's fees and the rest going towards the construction of the thousands of units that were to be built. When Harlequin collapsed into administration in 2013, facing a £1.2 billion shortfall in funds, fewer than 200 units had been built and they were all at the same resort – Buccament Bay in St Vincent and the Grenadines. In August 2022, Ames was convicted by a jury on two counts of fraud for abuse of position following a five-year SFO investigation. He was jailed for twelve years. The court heard how Ames and his family took £6.2 million from Harlequin and enjoyed a millionaire's lifestyle, jetting in and out of the Caribbean. Some family members were paid £10,000 a month. Even after a 2011 warning by insolvency practitioners that he might be trading while insolvent, Ames didn't stop selling.

Could investors have foreseen that there were problems with the development? It's easy to be fooled by glossy endorsements, but proper scrutiny of the contracts involved should have raised questions. For example, it would have revealed that investor funds were not ring-fenced for particular resorts or properties, but rather spread over the entire Harlequin business. The most significant sign that something wasn't right though, was that there was no other source of external funding. The growth of the operation was entirely dependent upon a large number of new investors signing up. To build one unit, Harlequin's highly incentivised sales teams (on commissions as high as 10% of the purchase price) had to sell three units. If it sounds like a pyramid scheme, that's because it was.

In reality, investors should have seen the red flags the moment they sat down to hear a presentation by Ames. It wasn't just that it was a little too slick. The numbers just didn't add up. The projections stated that there would be 100,000 visitors *a week* to the resorts (which is how the investors would achieve their rental returns). This would have equated to around five jumbo jets a day flying into the islands. Common sense should have indicated that this just wasn't likely.

Always check that the asset exists[47]

Recommending that investors ensure that an asset they put their money into actually exists might sound like obvious advice, but you'd be surprised at how often people take it for granted that they are being offered something real. This is the basis for the success of so-called 'boiler room' scams.

Often, the investments do sound compelling, as in the example of Essex and London Properties (ELP). In 2022, the company claimed to have bought several properties along the Elizabeth Line from London to Essex and had the plan to refurbish and sell them at a handsome profit. The soon-to-be-launched rapid and regular rail service would inevitably attract many new commuters, who might look for their dream homes a little way out of the Capital. On paper at least, it looked like an interesting investment. That's what more than 800 people thought when they made payments of between £5,000 and £140,000 to ELP. Many, after making an initial payment, even went on to increase their stakes. In reality, the team behind ELP had purchased just one single property in Harwich for less than 1% of the money they collected from investors. The rest of ELP's 'Elizabeth Line portfolio' simply didn't exist.

The scheme relied on boiler room sales tactics, where investors were cold-called and persuaded that this was a legitimate and compelling offer. Pre-recorded noise played in the background during the calls suggested that ELP telesales representatives were in a busy office. To add to the glossy facade, investors were sent professional brochures showing off some of the properties on offer. What they didn't know was that these brochures relied on photos stolen from estate agents' details. On one occasion, members of the ELP team even showed a wavering investor around a property they were looking to 'add to their portfolio' (which, of course, didn't happen).

There were no immediate signs that anything was amiss. ELP paid the first wave of investors interest on their investments. However, the money paid out was taken from deposits from the second wave. It was a classic Ponzi scheme. Overall, the fraudsters behind the ELP scheme pocketed more than £13 million before the scam was uncovered. Following an investigation by Essex Police, ELP was ordered into liquidation. In April 2022, following an eleven-week trial, four of the men involved with the scam were jailed for a total of nearly fifteen years.

Buying into an investment scheme via a cold call is never wise. The fraudster has the upper hand from the beginning and can direct the conversation in the way they prefer. In this case, the discussion was firmly directed away from the fact that ELP didn't own the properties in question. The boiler room nature of the call was also a big giveaway that this was a pressure-selling technique. Any out-of-the-blue offer that promises to make investors a ton of cash with virtually no effort is almost certainly a con.

If something looks off, it probably is[48]

Any well-heeled art lover would be intrigued if they were offered a package deal of four original pieces by Roy Lichtenstein, Keith Haring and Henri Matisse for the bargain price of $290,000. While a weighty price tag, that sum would still be very low for originals from such renowned artists. The problem is that in this particular case, the paintings were not originals. The so-called 'authentic' artworks, being sold by Galerie Danieli in an exclusive area of Palm Beach, Florida, were cheap reproductions that the gallery owner, Daniel Bouaziz, had bought from online auctions.

The scam was uncovered when one keen-eyed art enthusiast noticed that the sizes of some of the pieces did not match the originals and the edition numbers were incorrect. Further investigation found an identical copy of the Lichtenstein on eBay for just $535.50, a fraction of the cost of the one being sold by Galerie Danieli. After a customer complained, an investigation revealed a succession of works sold as originals when they were anything but. One buyer paid $85,000 for a 'genuine' Andy Warhol print, which turned out to be a fake sourced for $100 online. A Banksy was sold for $140,000 when Bouaziz had bought a replica of the work by the renowned graffiti artist for less than $520. After an investigation by the FBI, the gallery owner was indicted on mail fraud, wire fraud and money laundering.

When buying art and other collectables in their entirety, rather than on a fractionalised basis from established dealers, it is very much a case of caveat emptor ('let the buyer beware'). Investigating potential investments takes time, but weigh this up against the fact that the courts will be unable to help if an investor cannot demonstrate that they have acted reasonably in the first instance. A little bit of research about an artist and their work goes a long way. Well-known artists all have a catalogue raisonné (critical catalogue) which is a comprehensive listing of all the known artworks by an artist in a particular medium. Works are described in a way that means they can be reliably identified by third parties. There are also lost and stolen art registries such as The Art Loss Register in the UK and Lostart.de in Germany. Collectors should also ask for warranties to show that a piece of work is authentic with a good, clear title.

Don't just rely on the experts[49]

Even with access to comprehensive background details, it always pays when investors do a bit of their own digging. This next story has echoes of the Bernie Madoff tale, where several high-profile institutions missed the clear red flags. In this case, the suspicious firm was a Munich-based shipping container lease business called P&R. For many years, it was the darling of various banks and personal advisors so wealthy investors saw it as a safe bet to put their investment cash. For added peace of mind, there was the fact that P&R's annual accounts were signed off by the blue chip accounting group, Werner Wagner-Gruper. In 2015, they concluded that, 'In the course of our audits, no circumstances have come to light that would speak against the assumption that the company is a going concern.'[50] Who wouldn't be reassured by that?

As it turned out, there should have been very real concerns. In 2018, the business went bust. The insolvency experts that were parachuted in to sort out the mess were shocked at what they found. P&R was, in effect, running a huge shipping container Ponzi scheme.

To understand how it worked, we need to look at the origins. Businessman Heinz Roth set up P&R in 1975, based on the simple idea of inviting investors to put their money into buying containers, which were then leased out to shipping companies. Investors received rent on their containers and a guaranteed buy-back price when they wanted to cash out. Things began to go wrong early this century when P&R wasn't making enough on the sales, or leases, of containers to meet the rents it had promised investors. Somewhere around 2007, the business began using money from new investors to pay existing clients rather than buy new containers. The longer this went on, the more new investors needed to be found to pay rent to existing clients. By the time it all came to a head, P&R claimed to own 1.6 million containers which, as one commentator pointed out, was enough to stretch from Hamburg to New York if laid end to end. In reality, the business owned just over 600,000 shipping containers. Administrators warned at the time that, of the $3 billion invested into the business, a maximum of $1 billion was ever likely to be recouped for investors.

How, then, did the experts miss such a blatant scam? A large part of the confusion was down to the smoke and mirrors put in place by the P&R team. P&R's operations were split across operations in Germany and Switzerland. When a subsidiary in Germany wanted to acquire a new container, the money was transferred to Switzerland, where another subsidiary dealt with the purchase and leasing of containers. Even though P&R was skilful at hiding glaring holes in its accounts, it is fair to say that what was happening should have set off alarm bells at Werner Wagner-Gruper. An auditor in Switzerland flagged irregularities in the accounts, and checks could have been made on the inventory. Every shipping container boasts an ID number and P&R made lists of its stock publicly available. Someone should have been checking them more carefully. Likewise, Germany's financial regulator, BaFin, should have been more on the ball and asked critical questions of the business.

What this story tells us is that we cannot solely rely on others to do our job when it comes to due diligence. An investment that appears to have a reputable team around it and to have been signed off by partner organisations is not a guarantee that all is well.

Always investigate the principals[51]

If a crime is to be committed, someone needs to be behind it. In this case, it will almost certainly be the principal of the alternative investment platform: the person selling the investor the 'fabulous deal'. When weighing up an investment, one of the earliest, and easiest, checks to make is into the team behind it. Thanks to online resources from industry trade bodies to Companies House, it is a straightforward process to check on the credentials of individuals behind a fund. If a principal claims to have qualifications, licences or a spectacular track record, it is easy to check. Ditto, if they claim to have extensive experience in a certain sector. Just a few minutes spent online could prevent a serious misjudgement.

Such due diligence could have changed everything for investors who were duped into spending their fortunes on aircraft parts and leases that didn't exist. At first glance, it looked like the investment was led by a manager with industry experience and a cast-iron pedigree. San Antonio businessman Victor Lee Farias made much of his status as a registered broker and investment advisor with several securities licences. It was certainly enough to convince many retired police officers and first responders of Farias' credibility when he was seeking investment for his aircraft part leasing company, Integrity Aviation and Leasing. Farias raised $14 million from investors who believed the funds would be used to purchase engines and other aircraft parts which would then be leased to major airlines. Investors were promised interest at an annual return rate of 10% to 12%.

The leasing company did not purchase any engines and spent only a small amount on aircraft parts. While some money was diverted to make Ponzi-style investments to keep the money coming in, the rest went elsewhere. This included $2.4 million for Farias' expenses and $2.7 million to fund a friend's business. Even once the SEC began to investigate, Farias continued the scam. He used a copy of the letterhead on an SEC investigative subpoena as 'proof' for investors that he was working with the SEC to take the business public to repay investors.

Scrutiny of Farias' supposed qualifications revealed that all his securities licences had expired. According to checks, he had been associated with seven entities, many simultaneously, and some had been expelled by the financial industry regulatory body. He simply did not have the credibility he traded upon.

Distinguish between secured versus unsecured status[52]

Even when the rates of return might look hugely attractive, investors are always advised to thoroughly investigate investments to check on their status as investors versus all the investors in a fund. It is very easy to come unstuck if the extent of everyone's involvement is not immediately clear, and without this simple check, investors may find themselves at the back of a long queue if the investment does not go as planned.

This was the experience of a cohort of small investors who lost around £4 million on an investment into the George Best Hotel in Belfast thanks to their unsecured status. Each of the so-called 'bedroom investors' had stumped up tens of thousands to benefit from the leases of the hotel rooms once the Donegall Square development was completed and began welcoming guests. For many, the investment represented their entire life savings. Then, in April 2020, the firm behind the development went into administration when the building was still less than 70% complete. As is usual in such circumstances, the administrators sought legal permission to sell the unfinished hotel to fulfil its duty and distribute what proceeds it could to creditors. It was only at this point that the bedroom investors discovered that another lender, Lyell Trading Ltd, had been ranked as having the first charge over the property, having loaned a total of £8.36 million to the developers. As a *secured* creditor, Lyell Trading was first in line when it came to receiving a payout from the administrator. The unsecured investors lost their entire investment.

Before signing up for any investment, investors must always read the small print and check on what will happen should something go wrong.

Understand yield[53]

In a similar vein to the above, a little understanding of terms used in investing goes a long way. Investors need to know exactly what they are getting, because it is easy to be fooled by marketing material that seems to promise one thing, but is quite misleading.

If, say, you like a drop of the good stuff, or have simply read about the 500% rise in the value of rare whisky over the past decade, you may be tempted to invest. Googling something like 'buy whisky cask' will only add to the anticipation and excitement. Site after site will promise annual returns of up to 20%. While it sounds enticing, it's not as straightforward as it first looks. For a kick off, you do not get annual returns from a cask. That 20% is the average increase over the lifetime of a cask, not a year-on-year increase. It is only really possible to get that level of returns when buying a young cask and keeping it as a long-term investment.

Understanding yield, or income return, on an investment such as interest or dividends received is an important element of alternative investing. It is easy to get carried away by prom-ises of double-digit annual returns, but investors shouldn't take such numbers at pure face value. Investor naïvety over whisky investing has, at least in part, fuelled a burgeoning industry in slick-looking cask investment schemes advertising impressive returns but many investors don't realise they won't make any money until they sell their cask completely. One of the more recent cases involved a British seller arrested by the FBI for a $13 million scam where 150 US investors were lured in by promises of huge returns on investments in rare whiskies. High-pressure salesmen were said to have used aggressive and deceptive tactics, including using fake names and British accents to sound more convincing.

While there are undoubtedly significant profits to be made from investing in whisky, investors are advised to learn more about this asset class before committing their money (as they should with any asset class). There are many variables. The value of older casks increases more rapidly than younger casks, for example, and what is inside casks does not age indefinitely. There is also no simple way for a layperson to verify the value of a cask, which, of course, makes it easier for scam artists to manipulate the price.

It pays to familiarise yourself with investment terms and the lingo that is most commonly used in a particular sector.

Protection is not guaranteed[54]

No matter what the level of investing expertise, the final piece of advice is standard: always consult with a professional advisor. I will, however, caveat this with the advice to only work with a *good* and *trusted* financial advisor, preferably via a recommendation and someone with a discernible track record. Just as there are fraudsters out there who seek to relieve the unwary of their cash, there are also some unscrupulous, or certainly naïve, financial advisors. And, just because an investor has heeded the advice of a professional, it does not guarantee any protection should things go wrong.

Out of the more than 6,000 individuals who invested in a firm called Dolphin Trust, which billed itself as Germany's market leader in redeveloping listed buildings, many were encouraged to do so by their financial advisors. Dolphin Trust, which later changed its name to German Property Group, was embarking on a project to restore historical buildings and turn them into luxury apartments – a scheme which promised investors double-digit returns.

When the company collapsed in the summer of 2020, it owed more than €1 billion to investors around the world.

The majority of the investors were from the UK. What many didn't know at the time was that the financial advisors were typically paid a commission of 20% to 30% from Dolphin. Many investors complained that these same advisors did not make it clear that they were selling unregulated products, nor that it was a potentially risky investment. Since Dolphin was not authorised or regulated by the UK's Financial Conduct Authority (FCA), investors were not protected by the Financial Ombudsman Service or covered by the Financial Services Compensation Scheme.

Investors who are just starting out are vulnerable to poor financial advice like this. Once again, the only way to protect yourself is to spend time learning what good financial advice looks like. The onus is on advisors to lead with their credentials before they fully explain the pros and cons of any investment, which includes making clear any risks. Claims by an advisor that, 'This will make you rich,' or, 'Success is guaranteed,' are an obvious red flag. They are also obliged to disclose if they are getting any financial advantage out of making a recommendation. Anyone sceptical of the advice they receive should look at other options.

* * *

The message here is clear: unless you are an expert, or are working closely with one you trust, alternative investments can be risky. The industry is largely unregulated, so frauds, fakes, forgeries and knock-offs abound. You don't need to look far to find tragic stories of people who've spent huge sums of money only to find their investments worthless. However, with a lot of caution and due diligence, it is possible to largely protect yourself and your investment.

If you are still curious about alternatives after these protracted warnings, let's explore how you might get involved.

FOUR

What Do I Need To Get Started?

Deciding to bite the bullet and include alternatives in a portfolio is one thing. Quite where to start is another. The alternatives universe is huge, with an array of asset classes, investment styles, combinations, models and vehicles. There are also thousands of private investment funds and hedge funds and performance can vary wildly.

Establish your objective

The first step is as it would be with any traditional investment, and that is to decide what it is that you want the alternative investment to do for you. In other words, what are your investment objectives? (Having a firm plan like this will also protect you from 'impulse buying' an investment that just isn't suitable.) Think about what it is you most want from your portfolio, whether it is mitigating volatility, generating higher yield, protecting against inflation or all of the above. Once you understand more about your aspirations, it is easier to build a combination of investments that best answer these needs and to decide how much of your portfolio will be dedicated to alternatives.

Having identified your long-term objectives and, therefore, how much of your portfolio will be allocated to alternatives, and in which asset class, it is time to look more closely at your chosen alternatives to select the best products.

Choose a trusted advisor

For many alternatives, particularly of the established type such as private equity, private debt and hedge funds, investors are advised to work with a trusted provider. Previously, this would not have been an option thanks to the strict wealth criteria and the stipulation that investors are professionally qualified. It is now possible to invest with just a few thousand pounds via a new generation of platforms that pool funds, allowing investors to buy into private equity or hedge funds. Yieldstreet[55] and FundFront[56] are just two of many online platforms that allow investors to buy into certain private equity and hedge funds opportunities for a relatively small outlay. Other, similar, platforms open up opportunities in real estate investment trusts (REIT), private equity investment trusts, long/short funds and infrastructure funds.

Following what you've read here, getting started with alternatives is obviously not simply a question of choosing an investment vehicle. The priority is to find an established provider with your best interests at heart. No one wants to be steered towards unsuitable investments and the experts must make all the risks involved clear. The choice of provider is very much based on integrity, value and fit, but the other factor that cannot be overlooked is fees. Some established providers will promise much, but they will want some hefty fees to realise their strategy. These fees will eat into any accumulation of wealth. It is crucial that investors ensure they know what they are signing up for and exactly how fee payments are structured.

Some investors may decide they want to go it alone and many online marketplaces cater for such an eventuality. Suffice to say, the information contained in the previous two chapters shows this can be a risky strategy for anyone who does not entirely understand an asset class or the potential challenges around it.

Financial vehicles

For clarity, it might be helpful to run through some of the financial vehicles you may encounter in this market. The following five have all been around for some time and it is important to have a basic understanding of them as you plan your investment portfolio.

Mini-bonds

Mini-bonds, also sometimes known as high-interest return bonds, are typically issued by small companies, startups or businesses facing challenges raising capital from institutional investors. These mini-bonds offer investors a fixed rate of interest over a set period. The initial investment will also be returned to the investor at the end of the agreed term. The favourable level of the return reflects the higher risks involved in the investment.

Structured products

In this type of investment, any return depends upon an agreed set of rules, rather than whether the asset involved gains or loses value. An example might be where a product might only pay out if the index or market the product relates to achieves a certain level of performance over a specified period. Examples of structured products include guaranteed equity bonds, guaranteed capital plans, protected investment funds and guaranteed stock market bonds.

Venture capital trusts

Venture capital trusts (VCT) invest in small, new and/or growing companies that aren't bought or sold on a recognised stock exchange. The riskiest part of the investment is that the company may fail and, even if it is successful, the money can be tied up for *at least* five years. However, there are some tax advantages for investors.

Collective investment schemes (CIS) & unregulated collective investment schemes (UCIS)

As the name suggests, a collective investment scheme is one where contributions from several people are pooled into a single fund. Most such schemes are regulated by the FCA, but some are not, hence the name of this related alternative: unregulated collective investment schemes.

UCIS are generally deemed to be riskier than other pooled funds because they invest in assets that aren't available to regulated investments and so it is possible to lose some, or all, of the initial stake. There is also no investment or borrowing restrictions in the same way as with their regulated cousin. Since January 2014, the FCA has imposed restrictions on the promotion of UCIS due to the degree of risk they carry. They can currently only be promoted to certified high net-worth individuals, sophisticated investors and self-certified sophisticated investors.

Exchange traded products

Exchange traded products (ETP) are investments traded on the stock exchange that invest in underlying securities of assets. The most popular type of ETP is an exchange traded fund (ETF), which is regulated. Some ETPs can be quite complex. They might be bonds or have some other sort of more complicated structure, and these are not regulated, so generally have a higher risk. The value of ETPs rises and falls according to the value of an index (a group of companies used to measure the growth of a market) or another measure such as the price of oil or gold.

As greater numbers of non-professional investors enter the market, it is likely this list will expand and new and more innovative products will appear. We are already seeing the emergence of new fund structures such as shorter-term vehicles, open-ended funds which offer more options for redemption, as well as tokenised platforms. This will, in turn, inevitably bring more asset classes to bear and will see a further expansion to the family of alternative assets.

Key asset classes

In the following section, I will go through some of the other key asset classes I've mentioned before to cover some of the alternative options and platforms investors might like to consider when deciding how to balance their portfolios. It is by no means an exhaustive list, but it should give you enough to get started.

Aircraft leases

The uncertain economic climate has had an impact on the airline industry, with many major players unable to access bank funding to modernise their fleets. This has paved the way for alternative lenders such as AshlandPlace,[57] Castlelake[58] and Volofin[59] to provide much-needed liquidity in the market and growth in private equity investment funds. Other services that are more suited to private investors new to the market, such as Access Investments,[60] are expected to come online shortly.

Art and art finance

Traditionally, the buying and selling of artwork has been via primary and secondary markets. The primary market is catered for via galleries, which is where original pieces of artwork are sold directly to collectors. These galleries, mostly concentrated in large cities such as London and New York, are private businesses which represent a small number of handpicked artists. When a piece of artwork is sold, often for a substantial amount, the gallery is paid by taking a percentage of the sale price as a fee. The secondary market is represented by a network of auction houses, museums, dealers and retailers. The most high-profile works are sold by the most prestigious auction houses such as Sotheby's and Christie's, although there is also an established regional network of smaller auction houses. The auctioneers charge a percentage of the sale price for any piece of artwork, ranging from 15% to 30%, although there is a minimum commission fee. They also receive a fee from the seller for running the auction.

Fortunately, for private investors who are drawn by the potential of art, but put off by the large price tag for individual pieces, technology is beginning to transform the art market. Not only has the internet (social media, in particular) made it easier for lesser-known artists to show-case their work, but it has also greatly reduced the barrier to entry for those hoping to invest in art. As detailed earlier, tokenisation has given investors access to iconic artworks by artists like Picasso, Andy Warhol, Salvador Dali and

Jeff Koons, allowing investors to treat artworks as publicly traded assets through online platforms. I've already mentioned Masterworks,[61] but other established players that are worth looking at include Mintus,[62] Public[63] and Maecenas.[64] High-value paintings are (virtually) split into many thousands of tokens and each one is priced as a percentage of the whole. As well as giving access to an asset that may previously have been out of reach, there is the added advantage of liquidity. It is easier to buy and sell a fraction of an expensive artwork, and it can be achieved more quickly than hunting down a willing buyer for a piece that is worth millions. When secondary markets begin to emerge in earnest, it will make the trade in tokenised art more mainstream.

Collectables

Originally, any investment in collectables involved buying the physical item itself, often through specialist dealerships, in the hope that the item will increase in value. The landscape has evolved considerably and many individual categories of collectables now boast their exchanges and indices. This is far better for transparency, since specific comparisons can be made between similar transactions and performance benchmarked. There are, however, some types of collectables that are still relatively small and remain the domain of dedicated enthusiasts. Direct investment remains the only option here and this can be the riskier end of the market.

This is a diverse category, so before heading to specialist marketplaces, alternative investors might like to begin by checking on the Knight Frank Luxury Investment Index. This tracks the performance of a wide range of luxury goods and collectables and collates data from a range of industry sources.[65] Once you have some idea of where you would like to invest, you can move on to the various specialist funds, a selection of which I have included below:

- **Cars:** Investment platforms such as Car Crowd[66] and Rally[67] allow individuals to buy fractional ownership of classic cars such as the Ferrari F355 or Jaguar E-Type. Investors choose their car from a digital showroom and purchase shares. Investors, who can 'visit' their car on track days and at car shows, benefit from the appreciation in the car's price, as well as any dividends when it is used in paid appearances.

- **Sports memorabilia:** Collectable,[68] PWCC Marketplace[69] and Alt[70] are among several new trading platforms dealing with sports memorabilia, allowing investors options to buy items outright or buy ownership of a share. Each marketplace prides itself on checking the authenticity of the goods, as well as ensuring they are viable investments. Alt offers free, fully insured storage for graded sports cards.

- **Watches:** The limited supply of luxury watches has begun to spawn watch investment platforms, including The Watch Fund,[71] but it appears to be a volatile market because other platforms offering fractional ownership in top brands have come and gone.

- **Whisky:** With a recorded 483% rise in value over ten years according to the Knight Frank Luxury Investment Index, it is not a surprise that more funds are catering to the rare whisky market, including UKV International[72] and Vinovest.[73] Typically, platforms such as WhiskyInvestDirect help investors invest in quality whiskies at wholesale prices,[74] managing the long-term inventory of major distilleries. To combat fraud, a transparent online audit is maintained that publicly states ownership, where the cask is stored and the cask number.

- **Wine:** There are several investment platforms for the global wine trade, including Liv-ex,[75] Vinovest[76] and Cult Wines.[77] The funds vary a little, but essentially, investors declare how much they plan to invest, share their investment objectives and risk appetite and, once an account is opened, wine is allocated to an investor's name in a bonded warehouse. Investors can monitor their wine portfolio via client portals and gain access to additional benefits such as vineyard tours and events.

One final point to note on collectables. Lending is another option when it comes to profiting from collectables. Individual parts of a collection, whether wine, watches or, indeed, an entire portfolio of collectables, can be used as collateral to secure a loan. This is an option offered by many private banks, although usually an option only open to their high-net-worth clients. Loans raised against the value of a collection give an investor liquidity and/or allow proceeds to be re-invested into other income-producing assets. Lenders will, however, wish to value the collection and place a first lien upon it. They will also want to know the location and provenance of the collection.

Commodities

On paper at least, the most straightforward way to buy commodities, from gold to coffee and crude oil, is to physically buy them. There is certainly the advantage that there is no need to go through a third party. A simple internet search will locate a dealer and they will sell the commodity in question. Often, if the investor no longer wants that commodity, they can sell it back through the same dealer. Of course, the challenge lies in delivery and storage. It's relatively simple (although not fool-proof, thanks to security concerns) with something like gold or other precious metals such as silver, copper and palladium, where the amounts will be manageable and the investments could feasibly be stored in a safe place. Most people would be stumped, though, if they had to work out where to keep any meaningful quantity of soft commodities such as cattle, energy products like crude oil, or agricultural produce such as corn, soya or cotton.

Major investors trade commodity derivatives such as futures contracts, but a brokerage account is required. This requires that a certain amount of capital, or margin, is maintained in the brokerage account. The alternative for those who don't have brokerage accounts, or such deep pockets, is to invest in commodity exchange-traded funds (ETF) and mutual funds. Such funds invest in physical materials, commodities stocks, futures contracts or a combination thereof. It is worth noting that commodity funds may not move in sync with the rise and fall of the price of the actual goods.

Cryptocurrency

Despite all the headlines about Bitcoin million-aires, the direct purchase of cryptocurrencies in the hope that they will massively appreciate is a highly risky strategy. Not to mention, this buy-and-hold option can needlessly tie up investment capital which can be much better deployed elsewhere. As stated earlier, the true value of crypto lies in blockchain and its position as a public ledger that records transaction information. The capabilities of blockchain extend far beyond creating new units of currency. Big businesses are already experimenting with using blockchain to improve efficiency and grow profitability. Walmart has been testing out using it to track food distribution from its supply chain network, while Tesco is using blockchain technology to verify the recycled status of the plastic used in its packaging.

For the alternatives investor keen on the future potential of blockchain, there are a few options. You could go mainstream by investing in public companies like Walmart and Tesco that are involved in blockchain. Another strategy would be to buy an exchange traded fund that specifically invests in businesses with exposure to blockchain, such as Amplify Transformational Data Sharing[78] or iShares.[79] Alternatively, there are financial derivatives exchanges such as CME Group[80] that offer investors an option to hedge cryptocurrency exposure.

In all cases, think beyond Bitcoin and the potential meteoric rise in the value of individual currencies. Blockchain is a technology that will allow progressive companies to grow and unlock new value through more efficient processes. Taking time to understand the real implications around blockchain and which areas of our lives it will most impact is a great long-term investment strategy.

Intellectual property

For ease, it might help to segment the investment potential of the IP market into product areas, since the potential opportunities and providers are quite diverse.

Healthcare: In days gone past, large pharmaceutical companies funded the drug development process themselves. However, as demand for new types of drugs grew, outside investment became imperative and the concept of healthcare royalties was born. Under this arrangement, investors earn in several ways. Royalties, through funding the research and development of drugs, yield between 5% and 20%, depending upon the clinical development stage of a product.[81] Another strategy is for investors to extend loans to or to buy debt from healthcare firms that have patent-protected new developments, but lack the funds to go through the necessary stages to bring them to market, which is a lengthy process. In recent times, the opportunities for healthcare investment have soared, thanks to the growth in biotech. In the UK, the number of enterprises involved in research and experimental development in biotech has grown from 174 in 2008 to 1,293 in 2020.[82] There's an investment opportunity there too: the average growth in the share price of UK biotech is 32%.[83] Alternative investors will find several healthcare royalty models emerging for the burgeoning biotech industry, including Oxford Capital,[84] HealthCare Royalty,[85] Royalty Pharma[86] and Xoma.[87]

It is anticipated that there will be more interest in this sector as the entire healthcare industry is under pressure to respond to broader trends in demographics such as our ageing population.

Music: The concept of investing in music royalties is not a bet on who is going to be a big star. It's a lot more about track record (excuse the pun!). Typically, music publishing rights last for seventy years after the death of the last author involved in the composition of a song, so it is a long-lived asset. The signs are that music fans are listening to their favourite artists more than ever. Weekly music consumption averaged 20.1 hours in 2022, up from 18.4 hours in 2021, with an interest in more than 500 different genres from samba and disco to heavy rock.[88]

One of the plus factors to music royalty investment is liquidity. After the investment is made, investors begin receiving royalties within six months. The payout doesn't depend upon the artists, only on the fact that there are music rights. The key to success is often settling upon a mature artist who has demonstrated consistent sales over an extended period. Royalty streams can go up and down periodically in line with whether the artist is in fashion or not, but popular artists do tend to produce steady royalty streams. Events such as the death of an artist or when a track is used in a popular TV advert or movie can see royalties rapidly rise.

The new generation of online music royalty platforms such as ANote Music,[89] Hipgnosis Songs[90] and Royalty Exchange[91] rely on blockchain technology to store proof of transactions. Investors can choose from detailed music catalogues showing historical data, contracts and future income potential before placing bids in live auctions to own a fractional share of an artist's music catalogue. Shares can be subsequently traded with other investors.

Mining

When it comes to mining, whether it is oil and gas, minerals or precious metals like gold and silver, the initial outlay is huge. There are costs associated with exploration, drilling, storage and distribution. Traditionally, high-net-worth individuals have got in on the act by investing in royalties based on a percentage of the sales or production, thus benefiting from the revenue stream of an asset that is difficult to extract. Some assets also offer tax advantages such as lower capital gains. This market is catered for by a large number of private equity funds, mutual funds or ETFs that offer diversified exposure to a range of these elements.

There are signs that this market is broadening out to a wider range of individual private investors, thanks to tokenised investment opportunities. Gold has mainly led the way, with platforms such as Gilded[92] offering fractional ownership of the yellow metal. The idea is to lower the barrier to entry for interested investors to buy assets that may previously have been out of reach. Other tokenised assets in this sector are coming into view, but it is currently a matter of 'watch this space'.

Technology

Growth in UK tech has surpassed the $1 trillion milestone, making it only the third country to reach this valuation after the US and China.[93]

Once an asset class reserved exclusively for institutional investors, private investors now have access to tech startup investments. There are various routes to get involved, from directly purchasing shares from a company without any intermediary, to selecting opportunities via an online platform. Investments can vary, from a stake in a startup to a share in the IP or patent of a tech business. The platforms will do a great deal of the work of vetting tech companies against strict eligibility criteria and growth potential. Check crowdfunding platforms such as Seedrs,[94] Kickstarter[95] and Indiegogo[96] for investment opportunities to buy a stake in a tech business and, for a more specific invest-ment in a patented technology, look at what is happening with funds such as Magnetar Capital[97] and Vector Capital[98].

Life settlements

As it currently stands, major investments in life settlements are led by institutional investors, fund managers and family offices. There are some well-known advocates among this group, which include Warren Buffett's Berkshire

Hathaway Life Insurance Co, and Bill Gates, who is said to have invested more than $500 million.[99]

Private investors can get involved by either investing directly in life insurance funds or by putting money into private funds which repurchase policies that are about to lapse. Since the life settlement structure is quite complex, institutional and accredited investors generally invest via collective investment vehicles or public companies.

Litigation finance

For a long time, the main players in litigation finance have been independent law firms, in-house legal counsel, third-party aggregators and claim brokers. We are now seeing a lot of hedge funds and private equity funds enter the fray, attracted by returns that have been more than 20%[100] (although it should be noted that there can be a significant downside in the event of case loss). Multiple funds are also beginning to emerge that aim to raise money for litigation, some of which specialise in sub-sections of the market such as financial services or patent cases, or diversify on geographic lines. Opportunities for private investors looking to get involved in litigation finance include AxiaFunder,[101] Harbour[102] and LexShares.[103]

Shipping containers

The process of leasing shipping containers is not unlike renting an apartment. Investors rent a container and then receive a payment each month. The only difference is that there is no long-term tenant. Investors will be dealing with the world's leading shipping companies who are seeking to transport items around the globe.

There is usually a minimum spend required, such as an entry-level investment of around £9,000, which is equal to the cost of three 40-foot containers. The average life of a container is around twenty years, but most investment terms are much less than that (usually around five years). Investors buy the containers and then lease them back to a container company, which will rent them on to businesses wishing to ship goods. Businesses such as Container

Xchange[104] pay rent for the containers, which is returned to the owner of the containers.

* * *

When weighing up the most appropriate alternative investments for yourself, there are many variables to consider over and above pure risk. There is never a single 'right' answer for creating a diversified portfolio and none of us has a crystal ball to help us see how the market may change in the future. However, by carefully balancing your portfolio with a good mix of traditional investments and alternatives, and accepting that there may be some volatility along the way, you can increase your chances of growing and protecting your wealth.

FIVE

Managing An Alternative Asset Portfolio: The Core Principles

Ultimately, how much of your portfolio you decide to dedicate to alternatives is very much a matter of personal preference and appetite for risk. It is crucial to have an understanding of the background to all investments you make, but perhaps more so in the case of alternatives. You need to ask the right questions and be certain of your risk tolerance before you act. As this is a new asset class for many, the risks are undoubtedly higher. In this chapter, I will share ten core principles which will help you build a winning strategy that will increase your chances of meeting your goals, while reducing any potential downsides.

Ten core principles

1. Diversify

It is quite likely that you may feel quite passionate about one or more of the investments that are listed here. Maybe you are a huge Beatles fan and the idea of owning a stake in *Yesterday* by John Lennon and Paul McCartney would make your today, tomorrow and the day after that. (It probably would, too, since *Yesterday* is one of the top ten earning songs in history.) Perhaps you picture yourself living the jet-set lifestyle and wouldn't mind dropping into conversation that you own (a stake in) a private jet. Most people have collected something in their lifetimes, so there is a good possibility that you may be intrigued by making money from your one-time hobby. The problem is, to make money out of this asset class, you cannot allow yourself to be distracted by your personal interests. A successful alternative investment strategy is based on building an interest in a range of assets to spread risk and increase the potential for returns. The only way to do this is to become dispassionate about what you invest in and focus on the detail.

The goal here is to achieve a mix of products. In a traditional portfolio, this has meant a mix of large capitalisation stocks and investment-grade bonds, usually in a 60:40 ratio of stocks and bonds. More adventurous investors might include a wider range of stocks and bonds in their portfolio, including small-cap stocks, high-yield bonds or commodities, to diversify risk and improve returns. Investors (both individual and institutional) will also update their portfolio at least once a year to adjust for risk, depending upon their investment objectives or risk tolerances, or to reflect changes to the market which may make some asset classes more, or less, attractive.

An alternative investment strategy should mirror much of this. It is up to you to decide how much of your wealth you put into mainstream investments versus alternative investments and it will be very much down to your appetite for risk. The important thing is that you decide what proportion will be invested into alternative assets, and then work towards building a diversified portfolio. Remember that whatever proportion of alternative assets you choose to invest in should be a good mix of alternatives. You could say, balance more 'traditional' alternatives such as private equity and hedge funds with something a bit more unusual such as art, litigation finance and shipping containers.

The process of weighing up alternative assets is very similar to the one used for a traditional portfolio mix. The goal is for complimentary investments (ie, when one asset moves in one direction, another will most likely move in the opposite direction) to offset any potential losses. This isn't as simplistic as saying that one is safe and the other risky. Both assets may be perceived as potentially risky. However, if they are in different sectors or unrelated industries, it automatically decreases your portfolio's overall risk.

Other considerations when balancing a diverse portfolio are time horizon and liquidity. The time horizon is the amount of time you will most likely need to hold a specific investment. This can vary hugely in alternative investments. Liquidity is closely tied to the time horizon. If an investment has a long time horizon, it is considered illiquid, since the investor will not have easy access to their money for a long while. Alternative investments are often illiquid, because they are difficult to sell or take some time to fully accrue in value. You may like to think in terms of balancing alternative investments against the traditional elements in your portfolio. Stocks and bonds have no fixed time horizon, so are fully liquid.

2. Do (a lot of) due diligence

You only need to look at the hoo-hah around Bitcoin since it first appeared in 2009 to realise that the alternative investment market is prone to a great deal of mania. Bitcoin is not the first investment to create such an excited buying frenzy. It has happened repeatedly ever since Tulip Mania first emerged in Holland in the mid-seventeenth century. Tulips, which had been introduced to the Netherlands from Turkey a few decades earlier, were seen as beautiful, exotic and valuable. Suddenly, they began to be traded for ever greater sums. The rush to invest was led by growers and spread to investors, and then to ordinary people, who speculated that the price would continue rising. At one time, tulip bulbs sold for the same price as mansions on Amsterdam's canal fronts. The bubble burst when investors began borrowing large sums in the hope of paying them back with the profits from their investments. Many people lost everything as a result.[105]

It would be good to say that the lesson was learned, but history is littered with investment bubbles that have abruptly burst. The most recent is the collapse of FTX, the cryptocurrency exchange, once valued at $32 billion. When it crashed, it emerged that $1 billion in client funds was missing. And, as we saw in Chapter Three, there doesn't even need to be a bubble to catch some eager investors out. Mere promises of stratospheric returns are enough to get some investors reaching for their wallets.

There are many lessons to be learned here, aside from the adage, 'If it sounds too good to be true, then it probably is'. One of the most important takeaways from the tulip, FTX and various fraud stories is to take the emotion out of your investment strategy. It's very easy to get carried away when hearing about soaring investments as successful investors crow about their outlandish returns in increasingly colourful language. You may think, 'I can't miss out! If I hesitate, I'll be the one who looks like an idiot.'

Let me, for a moment, take the emotions away from it all by explaining a little of the background to the trend towards investment manias. When we find it difficult to avoid participating in the face of an outpouring of excitement and an overwhelming barrage of persuasive information, we go with the flow in a process known as 'herding'. Aside from the fact that I quite dislike the bovine implications of the term, it is clear such instincts do, indeed, encourage short-term behaviour. We saw this 'herding' instinct in the early days of Covid-19 when investors panicked and fled the markets and stocks suffered a dramatic global slump. Many long-term investors followed suit and their holdings suffered when the markets made an extremely rapid recovery. What our investments should, of course, be doing is supporting our finances for the long term.

Once you take the emotion out of the equation, your brain will be clear, which means you can do some proper due diligence. As we have seen throughout this book, there are risks and downsides to each asset class (as well as some unscrupulous players), so time spent on fully investigating the market and individual assets is time well spent. Whatever alternative investment takes your eye, it is prudent to thoroughly research and evaluate potential investments to ensure they align with your investment objectives and risk tolerance.

The due diligence questions every investor needs to answer include:

- What is the underlying liquidity of the investments? Many alternatives are highly illiquid. Even when an investing platform says there is a secondary marketplace or an option for cash outs, be sure to thoroughly investigate what this means in practice.

- Fees: Alternative investing platforms charge asset management fees that can be 2% or higher. Investors may also be liable to a seller's fee if they exit an investment early. Check all options.

- Contracts: Investors who are presented with contracts running into hundreds of pages should be on the alert. Yes, there needs to be a properly documented agreement, but when contracts are this long, it should set off alarm bells. What is the seller of the alternative investment trying to hide in there?

- Management: Some of the people or groups behind some alternative investment opportunities have a limited track record or experience. Due diligence must also cover the team offering an investment, or the platform hosting it, as much as the asset class itself. Google and the Companies House website are your friends here. Check on the background of all the individuals concerned. Launching, and then closing, multiple funds is a concerning sign.

3. Active management

Even if your due diligence has been exemplary, there is always a chance that something gets missed or will go wrong. Just as the stock market constantly changes, so does the status of alternative investments. Take the example of one mineral funding investment involved in gold mines in Australia and Tasmania. On paper, this alternative investment looked great and the team behind it checked out as legitimate. For the first few years, the returns were exactly as billed and investors must have been delighted. Then, unbeknown to all but the most diligent investor, there was an issue with one of the mines which meant it could no longer operate to full capacity. In response, the team behind the fund quietly restructured the debt in favour of a large corporation which provided fresh funding, giving it senior secured debt status. None of the initial investors were informed. As far as they were concerned, everything was looking good. Right up until it wasn't. The problems at the poorly performing mine turned out to be far worse than expected and dragged the whole business down with it, eventually forcing the holding company into administration because it couldn't meet its debt obligations. The first that most investors heard about this turn of events was when they were informed that the mining company had gone into administration. Unfortunately, this was also the point they discovered that they had no hope of securing any of their money back. Even if some investment cash could be recovered from the fiasco, they were second in line to the larger investor.

You could say that in a scenario like this, it is impossible to be fully aware of what is going on with an investment. The business behind it was behaving in an underhanded way by quietly finding new investors when things at one of the mines went sour. Here's the rub. The investment company's website actually trumpeted the second investment of the larger player. A glowing press release talked up the multi-million-dollar investment. Granted, the press release was light on the truth by stating that the injection was a cash investment rather than a debt restructuring, but it said enough for an on-the-ball investor to think, 'Hold on, what is going on here?' There was enough information in the public domain to prompt investors to ask questions and do some digging.

It is crucial to continuously monitor and adjust your portfolio to manage risk and ensure any investment is proceeding as advertised. If something doesn't look right, ask questions. If you don't get the right answers, ask more questions. And if you still don't get the answers you like, take steps to get your money out of the investment.

4. Make sure everyone's interests are aligned

One of the attractions of many alternative funds is there is close alignment between the managers of a fund and investors. In other words, the individuals or groups offering the opportunity have skin in the game and have invested a proportion of their own money alongside the financial input from outside investors. Often, there is also a high watermark, or peak fund value, which must be reached before the manager's performance fees are paid. This is a structure that can often only be found with alternatives, since mutual funds and traditional investments are simply not built in the same way.

In an ideal world, there will be a perfect alignment of interest between the investor and the manager. If the investment goes as expected, both sides will do well out of the deal. If it does worse than expected, there should be no possibility of one side losing substantially more than the other. We don't live in a perfect world, but ensuring that there is at least some parity in the outcome, whatever it is, is essential.

There is a balance to be had here. Private investors want their fund managers to be properly incentivised to meet the stated objectives and achieve the predicted returns. However, if the incentive is too lucrative for managers, they may be tempted to take extreme risks, cut corners, or not be entirely truthful about the progress of the investment.

If a straight high-watermark performance fee level feels like a bit of a blunt instrument, there are different ways to structure the agreement between management and investors. Managers could, for example, reduce the level of their incentives in return for investors agreeing to lock up their capital for longer. Discounts and rebates on management fees can be introduced on a sliding scale when assets rise above particular thresholds. There could be an agreement whereby performance fees are calculated and charged annually, rather than monthly, when profitable positions are closed out. Some fund managers will even agree to 'clawbacks', where a share of past performance fees is returned to investors during extended loss periods.

As alternatives become a more popular investment strategy, it seems inevitable (although not guaranteed) that fund-based investments will seek to align themselves with investor expectations. Even so, investors need to push hard for this and ask all the right questions.

5. A long-term perspective may be necessary

A good rule of thumb with any investment is, 'the riskier the opportunity, the longer the time horizon investors need to accept'. That way, if anything doesn't go to plan, there is enough flexibility built into the strategy to allow the market to recover from the setback and work towards realising a healthy gain. As stated time and again: alternatives are risky investments. *Ergo*, wise investors maintain a long-term perspective and are not likely to get caught up in a panic about short-term market fluctuations. Cutting short an investment by abruptly cashing out will almost certainly result in subpar performance and, most likely, a substantial loss.

The alternative investments highlighted in this book almost all require cash to be tied up for long periods, although time horizons do vary according to the specific asset. Private equity and venture capital funds can span for a decade. There may be payouts over that period, depending upon the nature of the fund and the agreed milestones, but the investor may not have access to their initial stake for several years. With other alternatives, the time horizon is not even certain and is wholly dependent upon market conditions. Real estate is the most well-known example of this. Think here of the slump in house prices in the year immediately ahead of the pandemic, which then soared in the post-Covid recovery period and dropped dramatically after that. Other alternatives, particularly art and collectables, share the same characteristics. Sometimes, almost overnight, an asset will be 'hot' and the moment will be right to realise the investment. With certain assets, it can take many years for them to become 'overnight successes'.

Don't lose sight of the fact that many alternatives will also take time to dispose of. Like real estate, physical assets such as art don't have a quick turnaround element and aren't always easily cashed in.

When weighing up the long-term time horizons for assets you'd like to add to your portfolio, consider them in terms of your unique circumstances. You may be close to retirement or be anticipating a significant life event such as buying a house in the next few years. If you tie up a large proportion of your wealth in alternatives, how will it impact these plans?

6. Manage risk

In this asset class, the payoffs are often asymmetrical. Losses are small, or limited to the initial investment, whereas the gains can be substantial, often several times the initial investment. Well, that is the intention, anyhow. In truth, there is still a risk and anyone who is in a position where they absolutely cannot withstand losing their initial investment should look at other, less volatile investment strategies. Even if you can withstand losing your investment, you need to do everything you can to manage the risk.

The first principle in this section was diversification, which is at the core of managing risk. It is such an important point, that I am now going to return to it and advise you to check your portfolio again. While, at first glance, it may seem you've done a brilliant job diversifying your investments by using a range of different assets and strategies, any additional time stress-testing your assumptions is time well spent. What would happen under extreme market conditions? Quite often, a diverse portfolio strategy falls apart during an economic downturn.

History has shown that seemingly uncorrelated investments act in rather the same way during extreme shifts in the markets, even though they were expected to react differently and were included in the portfolio to mitigate risks. During a period where there are sharp corrections and sell-offs, assets that were not believed to be vulnerable can be impacted. This is the moment investors discover that, unfortunately, they have not been as robust in their risk management strategy as they imagined. When weighing up how assets correlate, try to think beyond risks solely in terms of returns for the past few years. Work back to previous downturns and see how the various assets in your portfolio performed then. Past performance is no guarantee of future performance, but it can provide some important clues. Think also about how the various assets will behave in extreme market conditions yet to come. Consider a range of scenarios, from a market crash, to a political crisis, to a global health scare: in what way do you think your assets will react? Considering these conclusions, how does this impact the balance of your portfolio and the correlations between the various investments? If it doesn't seem quite right then adjust to better manage the risk.

7. Prioritise tax planning

Alternative assets are like any other assets when it comes to tax. If you sell them for a profit, it can trigger a tax demand. How much tax you pay will depend upon the type of asset involved, how long you have held it and the level of your income. Understanding the tax implications of each investment is an important part of your due diligence process and should be done *before* signing on the dotted line.

As a rule of thumb, it is the underlying asset that is generally the deciding factor on what benefit is available and appropriate. There are tax-efficient options for investing and it pays to consult the experts. Generally, you will save more than you spend on such an exercise, so it is always worth it. However, the onus is always on an individual investor to keep track of any expenses and losses which might be used to qualify for any future deductions on their tax bill.

It is worth checking on government schemes, too. There are, for example, several options that offer more generous tax relief to encourage investment in early-stage unlisted companies or, in some cases, listed companies with a smaller market cap. This would include ISAs such as the Innovative Finance ISA, which allows consumers to lend and earn tax-free interest via peer-to-peer lending platforms, and the Stocks and Shares ISA, which is effectively a 'tax wrapper' that can be put around a wide range of different investment products. There is also the Enterprise Investment Scheme, designed to encourage investments in small, unquoted companies, and the Seed Enterprise Investment Scheme, another of the government's venture capital schemes offering tax-efficient benefits to investments in small- and early-stage startups and venture capital trusts, where investments earn up to 30% income tax relief on the investment (provided the investor's income tax bill is larger than the relief). There are also options around inheritance tax relief where, if an alternative investment is held for a certain number of years, it will fall outside an investor's estate and therefore not be subject to inheritance tax.

Contrary to popular thinking, investing in offshore investment funds does not confer a personal tax advantage over onshore funds, because investment funds and collective investment schemes in general are perceived to be tax neutral whether registered on or offshore, so investors remain liable for their gains. However, an offshore fund does not incur tax, which could be passed on as an additional cost to investors. The reason why private equity funds and hedge funds gravitate to offshore jurisdictions such as Belize and the British Virgin Islands is to gain more flexibility over the investing and risk management tools and to make it easier to attract an international investor base.

Be careful about getting caught out on less traditional investments. The tax treatment for art and collectables can be complex. For a start, the tax authorities differentiate between those who are mere private collectors and those who buy and sell art to make a profit. If a collector is making commercial gain or, more specifically, *enough* commercial gain, they may reach the VAT threshold and be required to charge buyers VAT on the pieces they sell. The timing of any sale can have tax implications, too. Works of art held for one year or less are subject to personal marginal tax rates of up to 39.6%, while anything held for more than that period is taxed at the maximum rate of 28%.

Many alternative assets have been covered here, which means the class as a whole may be complicated when it comes to tax, because different tax laws apply to different assets and holding periods. If you don't have a good understanding of the tax implications of your entire alternatives portfolio, it could end up costing you more than you thought and eat into your returns.

8. Consider liquidity and the illiquidity premium

The liquidity of alternative assets does vary, which is why this is another consideration in building a diverse portfolio. Venture capital and loans are highly illiquid, while there is a little more room for manoeuvre with art, collectables and life settlements. Some art and collectables can be extremely liquid in the buildup to, or at the peak of, a bubble of interest in the category. The tokenised assets I've highlighted here will go some way to addressing liquidity issues in certain asset classes when secondary markets are set up to buy and sell fractional shares in a similar way to traditional stock exchanges. It is still very much a case of watching this space while the government and financial authorities work out the implications of such processes.

When weighing up the liquidity of each asset, think about the demography of the investment base. Factors such as the number of market participants, investor appetite for the particular class of asset, market structure and transparency over pricing will all have an impact on future liquidity. Unlisted securities are less liquid than publicly traded ones because of the absence of a centralised trading point, so this will also have an impact.

It is very easy to define alternatives by what they are *not* (ie, a traditional investment where capital can be easily realised). Again, balance is what is needed to create a healthy and high-performing portfolio. If you can afford to tie your wealth up for a while then you can benefit from what is known as an 'illiquid-ity premium'. Market volatility following a succession of financial crises has intensified investor interest in liquid securities that they can sell quickly and move on from when a downturn looms. This growth has coincided with a fall in yields for highly liquid assets due to a shortage of supply. At the same time, yields in less liquid assets have been increasing due to lower demand. This adds up to an illiquidity premium, which is an opportunity for those who can take advantage of it.

9. Timing is everything

At the time of writing, the investment market is looking quite bleak. Interest rates are rising, inflation is hovering at its highest point for decades, the geopolitical situation is unsettled (to put it mildly) and the public markets are under pressure. For individual investors, their thinking will inevitably shift towards protecting capital for the longer term. This is, of course, where alternative investments can shine.

The market conditions will not always be like this, though, and any investment strategy should reflect that. The point I am making is that timing is an important factor when investing in alternative assets. Every investor should be mindful of market conditions and the economic cycle when making investment decisions. For all the benefits of alternatives, there are drawbacks, too. In better times, it might be prudent to follow an entirely different strategy focusing on more liquid short-term investments, or certainly to redress the balance of a portfolio.

10. Professional advice

The final core principle of alternative investment is a version of the obligatory small print along the lines of, 'The value of your investment can go down, as well as up.' As this book has made very clear, alternatives are at the riskier end of the market. Even without the various criminals that have seized the chance to exploit the less well-regulated sector, it is an area of the market that represents a higher risk. Investors should always seek the advice of a qualified professional financial advisor or investment manager with proven expertise in alternative assets. These advisors will help you to navigate the complexities of these investments and develop a strategy that aligns with your goals.

Afterword

Throughout this book, I have encouraged individual investors to protect themselves by conducting extensive due diligence as they take advantage of the clear opportunity offered by alternative investments. As with any sort of investment, there needs to be an extensive understanding of the benefits and risks involved. Before pinpointing specific opportunities, retail investors should take time to educate themselves about the different strategies deployed by the private markets, so they can understand how funds are structured. For their protection, there needs to be a clear understanding of fees and expenses, as well as how performance is measured. This means getting to grips with the metrics and terminology used, the difference between primary and secondary investments and the elements that drive standout performance.

Yet, for this asset class to continue growing, and for more people to benefit from the opportunity, I also believe that there is a role here for the financial industry as a whole. I don't simply mean by ensuring all investments are clean and above board. That should go without saying. What I mean is that those companies, platforms and funds behind alternative assets should become active more in educating investors. Online resources are crucial so that investors can do their research, but there is also an opportunity for investment groups to run accessible events with presentations on how this asset class can become part of a well-managed portfolio.

Transparency will continue to be important, if not more so. Lack of data is an issue with any sort of investment, but with an asset class that has had a somewhat chequered history like this, funds and investment platforms must help less experienced investors become more comfortable with what is happening to their money. All investors require sufficient information with which to make informed decisions. While I can't yet foresee a time when private investment companies are required to disclose as much information as their public counterparts, I do believe we will see a significant move towards greater transparency over time. If this doesn't happen voluntarily, then it will eventually be mandated by law. We've already seen proposals by the US Securities and Exchange Commission to increase the 'transparency, competition and efficiency' in the marketplace[106] and moves from the UK's FCA to achieve something similar. One of the requirements under discussion is a requirement for private fund advisors to provide investors with quarterly statements on fund fees, expenses and performance.

It's a hugely positive trend that retail investors are, at last, being given more opportunities to access the alternative assets markets which were previously only available to the super-rich. It bodes well for those who wish to build a more diversified portfolio, offering the prospect of better returns even in a difficult market, albeit at a higher risk. The so-called democratisation of investment is still in its early days though, and this transition will only go smoothly if carefully managed by all parties.

It is inevitable that, with a wider pool of potential investors coming on board, we will see further shifts in the alternative marketplace. Investments such as hedge funds and private equity markets, once the exotic alternatives of their day, have already become more mainstream, not least because they've been subject to stricter regulations. This leaves an opportunity for a new category of exotic investments to evolve and eventually become more mainstream, from collectables, to art, to IP.

Much of the growth of exotics will be fuelled by technology, which will open this class of investing to an entirely new generation of investors through tokenisation. Technology has already opened the alternatives market to all investors, so pretty much anyone can begin trading and often with as little as £10. There is no longer the need to be an accredited investor or to prove you have thousands of pounds of disposable income. Caution is advised and, as I have said from the outset, new investors should always be wary of strangers offering 'unbelievable opportunities', but with a bit of careful due diligence, it is more than possible to build a decent portfolio which is cushioned from some of the hardest blows of today's uncertain market.

Notes

1. E Smith, 'UK inflation hits 41-year high of 11.1% as food and energy prices continue to soar', *CNBC* (16 November 2022), www.cnbc.com/2022/11/16/uk-inflation-hits-new-41-year-high-as-food-and-energy-prices-continue-to-soar.html, accessed 02 May 2023
2. G Wearden, 'Pound hits all-time low against dollar after mini-budget rocks markets', *The Guardian* (26 September 2022), www.theguardian.com/business/2022/sep/25/city-braces-for-more-volatility-mini-budget-rocks-pound-parity-dollar-bond-tax, accessed 02 May 2023
3. L Elliott, 'Britain the only G7 economy forecast to shrink in 2023', *The Guardian* (31 January 2023), www.theguardian.com/business/2023/jan/31/britain-only-g7-economy-expected-shrink-2023-imf, accessed 02 May 2023
4. B Carlson, '2022 was one of the worst years ever for markets', A Wealth Of Common Sense (2 January 2022), https://awealthofcommonsense.com/2023/01/2022-was-one-of-the-worst-years-ever-for-markets, accessed 02 May 2023
5. M Turner, 'Investors flee UK funds amid recession, pulling over £1bn from market', City A.M. (8 December 2022), www.cityam.com/investors-flee-uk-funds-amid-recession-pulling-over-1bn-from-market, accessed 02 May 2023
6. J Reid, UK stock funds lost a record $10 billion last year, new research shows', *CNBC* (6 January 2023), www.cnbc.com/2023/01/06/sell-offs-hit-uk-equity-funds-hardest-in-2022-as-esg-gained.html, accessed 02 May 2023
7. J Jackson, 'Best and worst-performing asset classes of 2022', Interactive Investor (6 December 2022), www.ii.co.uk/analysis-commentary/best-and-worst-performing-asset-classes-2022-ii526218, accessed 02 May 2023

ALTERNATIVE INVESTMENTS

8. L Daly, 'Alternative investments of the ultra-wealthy in 2022', The Motley Fool (26 September 2022), www.fool.com/research/high-net-worth-alternative-investments, accessed 02 May 2023
9. L Daly, 'Alternative investments of the ultra-wealthy in 2022', The Motley Fool, (26 September 2022) www.fool.com/research/high-net-worth-alternative-investments, accessed 02 May 2023
10. 'Modern Portfolio Theory: What MPT is and how investors use it', Investopedia (10 September 2021), www.investopedia.com/terms/m/modernportfoliotheory.asp, accessed 02 May 2023
11. 'Art as investment', Britannica (no date), www.britannica.com/topic/art-market/Art-as-investment, accessed 02 May 2023
12. 'Bank of America private bank study finds younger investors turning to alternatives, sustainability and digital assets to create wealth', Bank of America (11 October 2022), https://newsroom.bankofamerica.com/content/newsroom/press-releases/2022/10/bank-of-america-private-bank-study-finds-younger-investors-turni.html, accessed 02 May 2023
13. A Michael, 'What you need to know about alternative investments', *Forbes Advisor* (25 November 2022), www.forbes.com/uk/advisor/investing/what-you-need-to-know-about-alternative-investments, accessed 02 May 2023
14. CJI Team, 'Strongest private jet sales ever reported by IADA members', Corporate Jet Investor (19 January 2023), www.corporatejetinvestor.com/news/strongest-private-jet-sales-ever-reported-by-iada-members, accessed 02 May 2023
15. S Meredith, 'Private jet use is more popular than ever – and first-time buyers are driving record sales', *CNBC* (19 July 2022), www.cnbc.com/2022/07/19/private-jet-use-is-more-popular-than-ever-and-first-time-buyers-are-driving-record-sales.html, accessed 02 May 2023
16. E Saner, 'Flying shame: The scandalous rise of private jets', *The Guardian* (26 January 2023), www.theguardian.com/environment/2023/jan/26/flying-shame-the-scandalous-rise-of-private-jets, accessed 02 May 2023
17. *Aircraft Leasing Market Share, Size, Trends, & Industry Analysis Report: By lease (dry, wet); by aircraft (narrow*

body, wide body) by region, market size & forecast, 2022 – 2029, (Polaris Market Research, December 2021), www.polarismarketresearch.com/industry-analysis/aircraft-leasing-market, accessed 02 May 2023

18. 'This asset class has outpaced the S&P 500 for 25 years', AltExchange (16 May 2022), www.altexchange.com/blog/this-asset-class-has-outpaced-the-sp-500-for-25-years-2, accessed 02 May 2023

19. A Shirley, 'Art tops 2022 luxury investment index', The Intelligence Lab, Knight Frank (1 March 2023), www.knightfrank.com/research/article/2023-03-01-art-tops-2022-luxury-investment-index-, accessed 19 May 2023

20. 'The top 10 investment gemstones', The Natural Gem (23 March 2022), https://thenaturalgem.com/en/the-top-10-investment-gemstones, accessed 02 May 2023

21. *Virtual Currencies: Key Definitions and Potential AML/CFT Risks*, (FATF, June 2014), www.fatf-gafi.org/en/publications/Methodsandtrends/Virtual-currency-definitions-aml-cft-risk.html, accessed 02 May 2023

22. 'Blockchain by Cisco', Cisco (2018), https://masimatteo.files.wordpress.com/2018/07/blockchainbycisco_build-trust-based-business-networks-for-digital-transformation.pdf, accessed 02 May 2023

23. M Frankl-Duval and L Harley-McKeown, 'Investors in search of yield turn to music-royalty funds', *The Wall Street Journal* (22 September 2019), www.wsj.com/articles/investors-in-search-of-yield-turn-to-music-royalty-funds-11569204301, accessed 02 May 2023

24. 'Music royalties deliver 12.14% yield in 2019', Royalty Exchange (3 February 2020), https://royaltyexchange.com/blog/music-royalties-deliver-12-14-yield-in-2019, accessed 02 May 2023

25. *United Kingdom (UK) Life Insurance Market, Key Trends and Opportunities to 2025*, (Global Data, 25 April 2022), www.globaldata.com/store/report/uk-life-insurance-market-analysis, accessed 02 May 2023

26. B Russell, 'Almost two in five over-55s saw costs exceed income in 2022 according to research from more2life and the CeBR', *IFA* (22 January 2023), https://ifamagazine.com/article/almost-two-in-five-over-55s-saw-costs-exceed-income-in-2022-according-to-research-from-more2life-and-the-cebr, accessed 02 May 2023

27. S Von Imhof, 'Investing in litigation finance', Alts.co (8 May 2022), https://alts.co/investing-in-litigation-finance, accessed 02 May 2023

28. A Nagurney, 'Global shortage of shipping containers highlights their importance in getting goods to Amazon warehouses, store shelves and your door in time for Christmas', *The Conversation* (21 September 2021), https://theconversation.com/global-shortage-of-shipping -containers-highlights-their-importance-in-getting-goods -to-amazon-warehouses-store-shelves-and-your-door-in -time-for-christmas-168233, accessed 02 May 2023

29. Davenport Laroche, https://davenportlaroche.com, accessed 02 May 2023

30. 'Capital Markets Fact Book, 2022', SIFMA (12 July 2022), www.sifma.org/resources/research/fact-book, accessed 02 May 2023

31. E Aktug, 'There is no alternative to alternative assets: Diversifying into private markets can build resilience but expertise and experience are required', *Financial Times* (5 December 2022), www.ft.com/content/07324c3d-d7a5-4ef4-a724-33ce4625f67f, accessed 02 May 2023

32. 'Alternatives in 2022', Preqin (12 January 2022), www .preqin.com/insights/research/reports/alternatives-in -2022, accessed 02 May 2023

33. *The Mainstreaming of Alternative Investments*, (McKinsey & Company, June 2012), www.mckinsey.com/~/media /mckinsey/dotcom/client_service/financial%20services /latest%20thinking/reports/the_mainstreaming_of _alternative_investments.pdf, accessed 02 May 2023

34. S Tan, 'The global shipping industry is facing a new problem – too many containers', *CNBC* (10 November 2022), www.cnbc.com/2022/11/11/global-shipping -industry-faces-a-new-problem-too-many-containers.html, accessed 02 May 2023

35. 'What are the average returns of the FTSE 100?', IG (no date), www.ig.com/uk/trading-strategies/what-are-the -average-returns-of-the-ftse-100--200529, accessed 02 May 2023

36. J Maverick, 'S&P 500 average return', Investopedia (5 April 2023), www.investopedia.com/ask/answers/042415 /what-average-annual-return-sp-500.asp, accessed 02 May 2023

37. 'Understanding qualified investors and how to work with them', The Sumsuber (9 May 2021), https://sumsub .com/blog/qualified-investor, accessed 02 May 2023

38. B Kupec, 'The implications of democratized private markets', Moonfare (18 March 2022), www.moonfare .com/blog/democratized-private-markets-implications, accessed 02 May 2023

39. 'FCA Portfolio Letter: Our Alternatives Supervision Strategy 2022', FCA (9 August 2022), www.fca.org.uk/publication/correspondence/portfolio-letter-alternatives-2022.pdf, accessed 05 May 2023

40. J Segal, 'How regulators killed hedge funds', Institutional Investor (24 May 2021), www.institutionalinvestor.com /article/b1rzcg6gzgj8nt/How-Regulators-Killed-Hedge -Funds, accessed 05 May 2023

41. 'New study finds aggregate decline in hedge fund performance since 2008', Vanderbilt University (19 May 2021), https://business.vanderbilt.edu/news/2021 /05/19/new-vanderbilt-study-aggregate-hedge-fund -performance-decline-since-2008, accessed 05 May 2023

42. 'Is private equity overrated?', *The New York Times* (4 December 2021), www.nytimes.com/2021/12/04 /business/is-private-equity-overrated.html, accessed 05 May 2023

43. *U.S. Cannabis Market Size, Share & Trends Analysis Report By End-use (Medical, Recreational, Industrial), By Source (Marijuana, Hemp), By Derivative (CBD, THC), And Segment Forecasts, 2023–2030*, (Grand View Research, no date), www.grandviewresearch.com/industry-analysis/us -cannabis-market, accessed 05 May 2023

44. A Gibbons, 'Home Secretary "receptive" to calls to upgrade cannabis to Class A', *The Guardian* (9 October 2022), www.independent.co.uk/news/uk/suella-braverman-jonathan-ashworth-home-secretary-home-office-bbc-b2198981.html, accessed 06 May 2023

45. C Davies, 'Developer who turned Caribbean dreams into nightmares in £226m fraud,' *The Guardian* (30 September 2022), www.theguardian.com/uk-news/2022/sep/30 /david-ames-developer-caribbean-resorts-pound-226m -fraud-case-harlequin, accessed 05 May 2023

46. 'SEC charges Kim Kardashian for unlawfully touting crypto security', SEC (2022), www.sec.gov/news/press -release/2022-183, accessed 05 May 2023

47. 'Four fraudsters jailed for £13.7 million investment scam', CPS (26 July 2022), www.cps.gov.uk/cps/news/four-fraudsters-jailed-ps137-million-investment-scam, accessed 05 May 2023

48. 'Valuable art was sold at low prices. Prosecutors say it was a scam', *The New York Times* (1 June 2022), www.nytimes.com/2022/06/01/arts/florida-art-fraud-warhol-banksy.html, accessed 05 May 2023

49. J Luyken, 'The greatest Ponzi scheme in German history', The German Review (9 July 2021), www.thegermanreview.de/p/the-greatest-ponzi-scheme-in-german, accessed 05 May 2023

50. J Luyken, 'The greatest Ponzi scheme in German history', The German Review (9 July 2021), www.thegermanreview.de/p/the-greatest-ponzi-scheme-in-german, accessed 05 May 2023

51. R Freedman, 'SEC charges aircraft parts leasing company, CEO with fraud', CFO Dive (2 August 2020), www.cfodive.com/news/sec-fraud-Victor-Lee-Farias-Integrity-Aviation-Leasing/582721, accessed 05 May 2023

52. 'High Court of Justice in Northern Ireland Chancery Division Decisions', BAILII (14 June 2022), www.bailii.org/nie/cases/NIHC/Ch/2022/10.html, accessed 05 May 2023

53. P Walker, 'As rare whisky prices rise, so do scams and schemes', *Insider.co.uk* (2 August 2022), www.insider.co.uk/news/whisky-investment-scams-27635375, accessed 05 May 2023

54. J Kollewe, '"I was told it was as safe as houses": Savers owed thousands as firm fails', *The Guardian* (20 February 2021), www.theguardian.com/money/2021/feb/20/i-was-told-it-was-as-safe-as-houses-savers-owed-thousands-as-firm-fails, accessed 05 May 2023

55. Yieldstreet, www.yieldstreet.com, accessed 05 May 2023

56. FundFront, https://fundfront.com, accessed 05 May 2023

57. Ashland Place Finance, www.ashlandplace.com, accessed 05 May 2023

58. Castlelake, www.castlelake.com, accessed 05 May 2023

59. Volofin, www.volofin.com, accessed 05 May 2023

60. Access, https://accessinvestments.com, accessed 05 May 2023

61. Masterworks, www.masterworks.com, accessed 05 May 2023

62. Mintus, www.mintus.com, accessed 05 May 2023

63. Public, https://public.com/invest/alts, accessed 05 May 2023

64. Maecenas, www.maecenas.co, accessed 05 May 2023

65. A Shirley, 'Art tops 2022 luxury investment index', The Intelligence Lab, Knight Frank (1 March 2023), www.knightfrank.com/research/article/2023-03-01-art-tops-2022-luxury-investment-index-, accessed 19 May 2023

66. Car Crowd, https://thecarcrowd.co.uk, accessed 05 May 2023

67. Rally, https://rallyrd.com/collection/cars, accessed 05 May 2023

68. Collectable, https://collectable.com, accessed 05 May 2023

69. PWCC, www.pwccmarketplace.com, accessed 05 May 2023

70. Alt, www.alt.xyz, accessed 05 May 2023

71. Watch Fund, https://watchfund.com, accessed 05 May 2023

72. Whisky Investment – UKV International, https://whiskyinvestments.com, accessed 05 May 2023

73. Vinovest, www.vinovest.co/whiskeyvest, accessed 05 May 2023

74. WhiskyInvestDirect Limited, www.whiskyinvestdirect.com, accessed 05 May 2023

75. Liv-ex, www.liv-ex.com, accessed 05 May 2023

76. Vinovest, www.vinovest.co, accessed 05 May 2023

77. Cult Wine Investment, www.wineinvestment.com, accessed 05 May 2023

78. Amplify ETFs, https://amplifyetfs.com/blok, accessed 05 May 2023

79. BlackRock, www.ishares.com/uk/individual/en/products/328618/ishares-blockchain-technology-ucits-etf, accessed 05 May 2023

80. CME Group, www.cmegroup.com/markets/cryptocurrencies.html, accessed 05 May 2023

81. 'Healthcare royalties: A funding gap with opportunities', abrdn (19 April 2019), www.abrdn.com/en/capgemini/insights-thinking-aloud/article-page/healthcare-royalties-a-funding-gap-with-opportunities, accessed 05 May 2023

82. *Number of Enterprises in Biotechnology Research and Experimental Development in the United Kingdom (UK) from 2008 to 2020'* (Statista, 25 October 2022), www.statista.com/statistics/471435/biotechnology-research-and

-development-enterprises-uk-united-kingdom, accessed
05 May 2023

83. M Bhandari, et al, 'The UK biotech sector: The path to
global leadership', McKinsey & Company (3 December
2021), www.mckinsey.com/industries/life-sciences
/our-insights/the-uk-biotech-sector-the-path-to-global
-leadership, accessed 05 May 2023

84. Oxford Capital, https://oxcp.com, accessed 05 May 2023

85. HealthCare Royalty, www.hcrx.com, accessed 05 May 2023

86. Royalty Pharma, www.royaltypharma.com, accessed 05
May 2023

87. XOMA, www.xoma.com, accessed 05 May 2023

88. 'Fans listen to music more than ever – Key takeaways from
IFPI's "Engaging with music" 2022', ANote Music (18
January 2023), https://blog.anotemusic.com/fans-listen-
to-music-more-than-ever, accessed 05 May 2023

89. ANote Music, www.anotemusic.com, accessed 05 May 2023

90. Hipgnosis Songs Fund, www.hipgnosissongs.com, accessed
05 May 2023

91. Royalty Exchange, www.royaltyexchange.com, accessed 05
May 2023

92. Gilded, https://gildedco.com, accessed 05 May 2023

93. 'UK tech sector retains #1 spot in Europe and #3 in world
as sector resilience brings continued growth', GOV.UK
(21 December 2022), www.gov.uk/government/news/uk
-tech-sector-retains-1-spot-in-europe-and-3-in-world-as
-sector-resilience-brings-continued-growth, accessed 05
May 2023

94. Seedrs, www.seedrs.com, accessed 05 May 2023

95. Kickstarter, www.kickstarter.com, accessed 05 May 2023

96. Indiegogo, https://entrepreneur.indiegogo.com, accessed 05
May 2023

97. Magnetar Capital, www.magnetar.com, accessed 30 May
2023

98. Vector Capital, www.vectorcapital.com, accessed 30 May
2023

99. 'Berkshire Hathaway strikes again', Reliant Life Shares
(2014), https://reliantlifeshares.com/wp-content/uploads
/2014/05/berkshire-hathaway-strikes-again.pdf, accessed
05 May 2023

100. T Healey, 'Litigation finance investing: Alternative
investment returns in the presence of information
asymmetry', *The Journal of Alternative Investments*, 24(4)

(2022), https://doi.org/10.3905/jai.2022.1.155, accessed 30 May 2023

101. AxiaFunder, www.axiafunder.com/investments, accessed 05 May 2023

102. Harbour, https://harbourlitigationfunding.com, accessed 05 May 2023

103. LexShares, www.lexshares.com, accessed 05 May 2023

104. 'Need rent to own shipping containers? Full guide + prices [2022]', Xchange (2 December 2022), www.container -xchange.com/blog/rent-to-own-shipping-containers, accessed 05 May 2023

105. A Hayes, 'Tulipmania: About the Dutch tulip bulb market bubble', Investopedia (22 November 2022), www .investopedia.com/terms/d/dutch_tulip_bulb_market _bubble.asp, accessed 19 May 2023

106. 'SEC proposes to enhance private fund investor protection', SEC (9 February 2022), www.sec.gov/news/press-release/2022-19, accessed 05 May 2023

The Author

Phil is a serial entrepreneur with a wealth of experience in alternative assets. He is also an investor in businesses spanning technology, venture capital, private equity and real estate, working with only the highest performing partners. Phil is CEO of RTK International Holdings, a Hong Kong-based financial services and commodities trading group, operating in four continents. He is the author of acclaimed books *Gold Rush 2020*, *The Last Dollar*, and *The Great Stagflation*, also published by Rethink Press.

You can connect with Phil Taylor-Guck via:

⊕ www.createtheobvious.com

⊞ www.linkedin.com/in/phil-taylor-guck
-1ba691198